The Dying and the Bereaved Teenager

The Dying AND The Bereaved TEENAGER

Edited by

JOHN D. MORGAN, PhD

The Charles Press, Publishers
Philadelphia

Library of Congress Cataloging-in Publication Data
The Dying and bereaved teenager /John D. Morgan, editor.
   p.   cm.
   Includes bibliographical references.
   ISBN 0-914783-44-0 : $16.95
   1. Bereavement in teenagers.   2. Teenagers and death.   I Morgan, John D., 1933-
   BF724.3.G78D95 1990
   155.9'37'0835—dc20   90-35058
                                                                                                                        CIP

This book or any parts thereof may not be used or reproduced in any manner without the written
permission of The Charles Press, Publishers, Inc.
The Charles Press, Publishers
Post Office Box 15715
Philadelphia, Pennsylvania
19103

ISBN: 0-914783-44-0 (paper)

Contents

PART III: The Role of the School in Dealing with Bereaved Teenagers

Contributors

David W. Adams, MSW, professor of Social Work, Chedoke-McMaster Hospital, Hamilton, Ontario.

Louise Allen, manager, Windsor, Ontario branch of the Canadian Mental Health Association.

Grant Baxter, B.Ed, head of Counseling Services, Lorne Park Secondary School, Mississauga, Ontario.

Helene A. Berman, MS, RN, associate professor of Nursing, Faculty of Nursing, University of Western Ontario, London, Ontario.

Sharon L. Cobb, MA, Health Educator, Ypsilanti Public Schools, Ypsilanti Michigan.

Catherine E. Cragg, M.Ed, assistant professor of Nursing, Faculty of Nursing, University of Western Ontario, London, Ontario.

Betty Davies, RN, PhD, associate professor of Nursing, School of Nursing, University of British Columbia, Vancouver, British Columbia

Eleanor J. Deveau, RN, BScN, nurse in the adolescent cancer unit of Chedoke-McMaster University, Hamilton, Ontario.

Sandra L. Elder, M.Ed, clinical psychologist in private practice, Victoria, British Columbia.

Kathryn Hustins, MN, RN, associate professor of Nursing, Memorial University School of Nursing, St. John's, Newfoundland.

Colleen Kelly, BN, RN, nurse with the Health Sciences Center, St. John's, Newfoundland.

Antoon A. Leenaars, PhD, C.Psych, clinical psychologist in private practice, Windsor, Ontario.

Lynne Martins, BA, grief therapist in private practice, Los Angeles, California.

Alicia M. Sims, high school student, Louisiana.

Robert G. Stevenson, EdD, co-chair, Columbia University Seminar on Death; Instructor of Death Education Programs at River Dell High School, Bergen Community College, and Fairleigh Dickinson University, New Jersey.

Wendy Stuart, RN, school nurse at Lorne Park Secondary School, Mississauga, Ontario.

Duane Weeks, MA, funeral director, Enumclaw, Washington.

Susanne Wenckstern, MA, clinical psychologist in private practice, Windsor, Ontario.

Introduction

Perhaps one of the most dangerous myths current in North America is that of believing youth is a time of blissful ignorance, that young people are unaware of responsibility, pain, and death. In reality it is unlikely that any child will grow into his or her teens without experiencing the pain of loss, the suicide of a friend, or the death of a significant other. One effect of the myth is to deny the teenager the opportunity to grieve, and thereby to assimilate the loss into the framework that gives meaning to his or her world. Another effect of this myth is to force the pain to manifest itself in violence toward self or others.

This volume is intended to provide caregivers, teachers, counselors, social workers, clergy, nurses, and administrators with a tool for helping teenage students through perhaps the most difficult part of growth, the acceptance of pain and loss. The authors represent a cross-section of caregivers: a physician, a funeral director, social workers, counselors, teachers, nurses, and grief therapists. The information they provide, the result of years of concrete experience, should be valuable to all who take the time to read this volume.

The book is divided into three sections. The first deals with seriously ill or dying teenagers, the second with bereaved teenagers, and the third with protocols that schools might adopt or adapt for helping young people in trouble.

David Adams' chapter "Care of the Child and Family When a Child Dies of Cancer," follows from his work at the McMaster Medical Center in Hamilton, Ontario. Mr. Adams, one of the few persons without a medical degree to hold the rank of full professor in a medical school, examines the feelings and needs of the dying child, the parents, and the siblings. His chapter concludes with concrete suggestions for helping children and families deal with loss. Colleen Kelly and Kathryn Hustins chronicle the development of an oncology support group for teenagers—Candles for Hope—and explain how to establish such a support group as an effective tool for seriously ill teenagers.

1

The second section of the book deals with the bereaved teenager. Alicia Sims, herself a teenager, writes of the joy she shared with her younger brother and the pain that she still feels twelve years after his death. Louise Allen, who manages a branch of the Canadian Mental Health Association, provides a concrete protocol for interviewing and assessing bereaved persons.

Helene Berman and Catherine Cragg discuss communication patterns within families and how the death of a parent can either aggravate the negative aspects of those communication patterns or draw upon the positive aspects to strengthen the family's bonds. Lynne Martins, a bereavement counselor in Australia, describes the long- term effects that the death of an alcoholic parent can have on a child, carrying through the theme of effective communication patterns discussed by Cragg and Berman.

Eleanor Deveau and Betty Davies examine the effect that the death of a sibling has on a teenager, Mrs. Deveau in an immediate setting and Dr. Davies from the standpoint of long-term follow-up. Sandra Elder describes the effects of loss on the completion of developmental growth tasks such as socialization, independence, sexual identity, and responsibility.

Duane Week's chapter discusses how the funeral director might help children of all ages; it is included because of the practical suggestions he has for helping teenagers.

The third section of this volume is particularly addressed to school supervisors, teachers, and counselors. It deals with protocols and programs that might be instituted to help young people deal with losses, especially with the losses that follow from suicide.

This is the first volume jointly published by the Charles Press of Philadelphia and King's College of London, Ontario, which, since 1975, has been a leader in the field of education about death and bereavement.

John D. Morgan, PhD
Professor of Philosophy
Coordinator of Death Education Conferences
King's College
London, Ontario Canada

Part I
The Dying Teenager

1

When a Child Dies of Cancer: Care of the Child and the Family

David W. Adams, MSW

When asked to write about the care of children dying of cancer and their families, I began by exploring my personal beliefs as to the proper care and found myself faced with several complex questions.

1. I believe that terminal care should be planned, but when can we say that a child is dying? Some children rally and get better for a while. Some children die unexpectedly; others experience prolonged deaths. How do we plan?
2. I believe that care should be continuous and given by those who know the child best, but should a pediatric oncology team, which may already be overburdened, do this?
3. I believe that children have the right to be comforted, to be children, and to make choices. Some parents cannot give up their searches for cure. Others place the dying child's needs second to those of the family or second to their cultural beliefs. How do we help parents without compromising the rights and needs of their dying child?
4. I believe that siblings should be involved in planning and participating in terminal care, but who involves them and when?
5. I believe that families need the freedom of choice to decide where a child dies, but do they always get it? What happens if resources are inadequate or not available?
6. I believe that dying at home in familiar surroundings is better for children, but is it realistic and feasible for all children and their families?

This chapter is an exploration of possible answers to these questions. In it I

3

will: (a) examine what we need to know, as clinicians, in order to work with these children and their families; (b) look at the feelings and needs of dying children, their parents and siblings; and (c) consider the respective benefits and shortcomings of home care and hospital care.

Childhood Cancer

There is nothing more difficult for parents than facing the death of their child. With childhood cancer, families are faced with uncertainty from the time of diagnosis: "Will our child survive?" "Can life ever be the same again?"

Fortunately, cancer is a disease for which survival rates are improving. Increased knowledge in every facet of treatment has provided a real opportunity for extended remission and cure (Adams 1979; Adams and Deveau 1984, 1988). Perhaps that is why death, when it does come, is seen by both families and caregivers as being so unjust and unfair. Such a struggle with treatments, the possibility of cure, and then death—everyone feels cheated. One father said:

> I am so tired . . . the struggle, the pain, the hope. We never believed this time would come. Now there is nothing to do except to wait. Can we make it through? Are we really strong enough to face our child's death?

When cure is no longer possible, we need to focus on providing palliative care for these children and their families. The work of Corr and Corr (1985), makes clear that our aim should be to maximize the quality of life for the child and the family. Our goal should be to allow the child and his family to live as well and as long as possible in their customary setting. To best achieve this goal, we need the answers to the following questions:

1. Dying Children. We need to know the personal characteristics of dying children, their place in the family, the roles that they play, and their stage of development. Children's cognitive capabilities will determine their level of understanding and their ability to cope. Their likes, dislikes, and individual strengths are major factors in determining their ability to face the difficult and limited time remaining.

2. Family Composition. We need to understand the composition of these families. Is it the family's only son or daughter that is dying? Factors including the roles and functions of individual members, the number of siblings and their ages, and the presence of extended family in the home will influence the ability of family members to cope and support each other.

3. Communication. Is the pattern of communication in the family open or closed? Spinetta (1977, 1978) found that if parents established a pattern of open and honest communication in the family, then their children were better equipped to face both good and bad events during their illness. Also, the natural pattern of distancing between dying children and their families prior to death was found to be less pronounced in families who communicated openly. Silent and anxious parents tend to create an atmosphere wherein the children are not comfortable asking questions or expressing their concerns. How do family members support each other if they do not talk with one another?

4. Cultural and Religious Beliefs. Cultural and religious beliefs influence families' behavior, their reactions, and their ability to cope. These beliefs may provide comfort or create added anxiety. Some customs prohibit the inclusion of children in decision making concerning their care. This will have a direct influence on the pattern of communication in the family as well as on the expectations of staff who care for the dying child. Cultural and religious beliefs may also affect decisions concerning further treatment, pain control, and care at home or in the hospital. We must identify the role of these beliefs early in the illness and work with families so that their child's care is not jeopardized.

5. Support Systems. Are family members committed to each other? Is there extended family nearby and are they a support or a burden? Chesler and Barbarin (1987) note that some grandparents and relatives are not helpful because they themselves are having such a difficult time coping with the situation. Are there other sources of support, such as friends or neighbors, that have been helpful to this family? Can they be mobilized to provide relief and assistance during this crisis?

Are employers understanding and tolerant of the demands of this illness? Can they be flexible enough to allow parents time to be with their dying child?

6. Social Problems. Are there any social problems such as financial difficulties, unemployment, or excessive use of alcohol or drugs? It is understandable that chronic illnesses can easily amplify any existing difficulties.

Environmental limitations, such as a lack of space, may impede caring for the child at home. Can we coordinate services and adapt the environment to accommodate the dying child?

Is the parent single, separated, divorced, widowed, or remarried? My experience indicates that single parents often have a very difficult and stressful time (Adams and Deveau 1984, 1988). As one mother pointed out:

> . . . if I turn to my parents I feel like I'm 17 again. I can't overload my 16-year-old daughter Suzie with my problems . . . I cannot go back to my ex for help . . . it's hard to know where to turn . . .

7. *Previous Experiences with Illness*.   What previous experiences, if any, have family members had with illness and death, and will these help or hinder them? There is no question that past events will have a bearing on how well families come to terms with their present situation.

8. *Parent Participation*.   The demands of this illness will tax most marriages. Are parents able to work together and share in the decision making? During the terminal phase, are parents able to be involved in their child's care or are they distancing themselves in anticipation of their child's death? We need to recognize the difficulties parents face as they try to maintain a balance between nurturing and emotionally smothering their dying child (Hamovitch 1964; Adams and Deveau 1988).

Are single parents able to cooperate with their estranged spouses to help their dying child? Or is the relationship a source of tension, anger, and frustration, with the dying child caught in the middle?

9. *Prognosis and Illness Cycle*.   If the prognosis for a child's cancer has been guarded from the beginning, families may have encountered many difficulties arising from the illness and its treatment. What have they experienced so far? What are their current levels of stress and fatigue? Are there any characteristics of this particular type of cancer, such as bodily distortions, that will make terminal care even more distressing?

Feelings of Dying Children

Children are as different in dying as they are in living. Dr, Mark Greenberg (1988), a pediatric oncologist, points out that the caregiver should not expect the stereotyped behavior of the dying child obviously suffering in pain and agony. Some children are resilient and playful even when their life is ending. They may be like 8-year-old Peter, who was flying his kite with his Dad at suppertime and died before morning, or like 6-year-old Carol, who clung to life through weeks of distress and pain before she died.

Dying children experience a wide range of feelings:

Fear.   Their fear may increase with final attempts to control the disease. This may mean (a) invasive procedures such as blood transfusions; (b) further surgery with possible physical changes; and (c) intensive chemotherapy that includes more side effects and pain. All of these measures are frightening and may raise their anxiety level.

Anxiety.   During terminal care, anxiety may be manifested in the following ways:

1. Young children experience separation anxiety when they must be hospitalized yet again. Separation from mother as well as from familiar surroundings has a profound impact on these children.
2. With older children, mutilation anxiety may prevail as they face further invasive procedures, experience bodily changes, endure physical deterioration, and suffer increased pain.
3. Children may sense increased anxiety in their parents and caregivers and this, in turn, may heighten their own apprehensions.

Anger. The anger of dying children may be directed at the disease, their parents, caregivers, themselves, or God. They might have had every reason to believe that they would get better with treatment. Now they may feel cheated—their trust in their parents and physicians is shaken as their disease progresses. They may be angry at the disease itself, for the control that it has assumed over their bodies and their lives. Physical limitations, increased pain, and isolation from family, friends, and activities may heighten their frustration. These imposed changes and restrictions are especially difficult for adolescents who have a strong desire for increased independence and the freedom to make their own choices.

Angie, age 16, was angry that her disease was out of control and furious that she needed to depend on transfusions to maintain her strength. She complained bitterly to everyone about what the physicians were putting her through. She finally refused to cooperate unless she was part of the decision making concerning her care, including the right to decide when she could not tolerate further treatments.

Sadness. These children have every right to feel sad and to mourn the loss of what they were and what they had before they became so ill. Losses and changes that they may experience include decreased contact with friends, reduced attendance at school, restricted participation in or absence from social activities, limited energy and mobility, changes in body image, feelings of discomfort or pain, and privation of security and hope for their future. No wonder that these children may be sad.

Loneliness and Isolation. Dying children are prone to increased feelings of loneliness and isolation as a direct result of the disease and the need for frequent hospitalization. Limited communication is also a major contributing factor. When important information is restricted or overlooked by parents and caregivers, children may be left on their own to interpret what is happening.

Peter, aged 11 years, was very upset when he was sent home from the hospital without an explanation. He felt that he was being sent home to die. In reality, he had improved enough that the physicians believed that he could benefit from some time at home.

If communication in families is closed, children may be excluded from detailed knowledge of their disease and its implications. When communication is limited there might be no opportunity for parents and dying children to share their concerns and fears and provide comfort, security, and reassurance to each other.

> Denise was 14. Her parents never openly talked with her about her disease and prognosis. When the physician told Denise about her impending death, she responded only by crying. Though hospital staff encouraged Denise's parents to speak with her, they were unable to do so. She died without sharing her feelings with anyone.

Needs of Dying Children

Love, Security and Reassurance. The need for love and security is fundamental to all children but is especially crucial to dying children in order to balance out their difficult feelings. These children need reassurance in the form of consistent emotional support, but they also need limits set on their behavior so that they know where they stand and feel more secure (Adams 1984). We should help parents to provide love and security even when they are in conflict and their lives are in turmoil.

Dying children need our understanding and acceptance as they try to contend with their fear and anxiety. They need reassurance that parents and caregivers will not judge them or retaliate against them for their actions and behavior.

> Nine-year-old Beth would lash out at clinic staff with her fists. They accepted her aggression, and when she was dying, she wanted them to be close so that she could hold their hands.

Honesty and Knowledge. Dying children often know more than parents think they do. If parents are able to be open and honest and share their own beliefs and feelings, it may help to decrease their child's anxiety, and encourage discussion. Parents may require our support and assistance to maintain their honesty as death may be so frightening that it heightens their need to protect their child from any further suffering.

Control. There are so few areas where dying children can have any control that allowing them to make some choices is very important. Choices may simply involve selecting the type of food they prefer or determining, within medically sound limits, when they receive their next injection. For older children and adolescents, choices may involve their participation in sports or other activities, even if such involvement is very limited.

> At 17, Ted had been a superb athlete. When his physical condition deteriorated from disease, he chose to continue surfing, even though he found it physically exhausting. It was his way of controlling his life. His father was concerned that he might injure or kill himself. However, his mother felt that "he would at least die happy."

We should help families to be flexible enough to allow dying children to continue to go on living.

Physical outlets and diversions may help these children release their anger and frustration constructively. Activities such as music, crafts, and outings with friends can be helpful and provide needed respite, especially for older children and adolescents. We should be creative enough to see that these opportunities are available.

Privacy.   Physical changes and deterioration may enhance the need for privacy, especially for adolescents. As they become more self-conscious of any changes and of their dependency on others, they require that we respect and accommodate their need for privacy. For example, Karen, a 16-year-old with osteogenic sarcoma, set clear rules for visiting. Only those who were closest to her were allowed to see her without her wig.

Before I address the needs and feelings of parents and siblings, I would like to stress the following key issues:

1. There comes a time when we need to focus on care rather than cure. If we think back to the *aim* of palliative care, we need to strive for optimal care when cure is no longer possible.
2. Time at home to be with the family in familiar surroundings is very important to dying children and should be our *goal* in palliative care, wherever possible.
3. It is absolutely essential to reduce suffering caused by pain. However, I believe that children must not be sedated to such an extent that they are unable to function or participate in the world around them. Pain must be controlled and, if possible, prevented. The best medical care can be complemented by measures such as warm baths, gentle rubs, and diversions that help to break the pain cycle.
4. Time is important, but what we do with that time is even more important. Allow dying children to do as much as they are able to do. I will always remember the seven-year-old boy who insisted on going to play T-ball in his last week of life. Children need to continue to belong and to be like other children.

5. What are the ethical considerations? Should dying children have further aggressive treatments? Is it necessary to continue with radiation, blood tests, and transfusions? Should children be included in this decision making? These questions need to be addressed and discussed. Children usually know when they have had enough and they will let you know. An eleven-year-old boy drew up a Bill of Rights and demanded that he be allowed to stop chemotherapy and die in peace.

Parents' Feelings

There is no doubt that parents of dying children have an extremely difficult time coping with the intensity of their feelings. Some parents believe that they are living a bad dream, hoping that they will wake up and everything will be all right again. Many find that they are on a roller coaster of feelings, feelings they have experienced in varying degrees throughout the course of their child's illness. They continually struggle with the reality of their situation and experience the following:

Denial.   There still remains the need to deny what is happening.
"This cannot be happening to us . . . to our child."
"Maybe this is just a phase of the illness that will improve and remission will come again?"
"Maybe the drugs will work better this time."

Denial may serve as a means of protection by temporarily alleviating intense feelings of anxiety, anger, and sadness. Fleeting periods of denial may provide much-needed respite from continuing stress. However, parents may require our assistance to face the reality of their child's death.

Sadness.   Parents are often overwhelmed with sadness because their own hopes and dreams for their child are shattered. This disease will not allow their child a future, a time to grow up and achieve his or her dreams. They are saddened by their child's suffering; often they find the physical changes alarming. We must recognize that there is a clear distinction between sadness and clinical depression. We must understand and acknowledge parents' right to be sad. As one father put it:
"I know that Penny will be in peace and that it's best for her, but I will never hold her in my arms and comfort her again. . . ."

Anger.   Parents' anger may be profound at this time. It may be directed at themselves, each other, the health care team, extended family, and God. They may question whether everything possible has been done to try to save their child, and if the physicians really know what they are doing. Occasionally, they may struggle with anger that is directed at the dying child for becoming ill and dying.

Guilt. Parents' inability to fulfill their inherent need to protect their child may create intense feelings of guilt. I have yet to encounter the parent of a dying child who would not do anything to avoid their child's suffering. Parents often feel guilty that disease has returned—they feel in some way responsible for the failure of treatment. They may also feel guilty for their irrational anger toward the dying child.

Loss of Control. Parents experience a tremendous loss of control over their lives; they believe that the disease has taken over their family life and they feel very helpless. When life is out of control, there are greater opportunities for conflict both within the family and between staff and parents. We must help parents to be clear about areas where they can maintain a level of control and areas that we, the clinical caregivers, are better equipped to handle.

Isolation. When families are caring for a dying child, they frequently feel very much alone and isolated. Friends and relatives may feel helpless, uncomfortable, or extremely anxious. Sometimes they withdraw or stay away from the family simply because they do not know what to do or say. Parents should be encouraged to maintain contacts outside of their home in order to decrease their sense of isolation.

Hope. Parents' hopes vacillate between the hope that they will be able to face what lies ahead and that their child will not suffer, to the hope that somehow a miraculous breakthrough will provide a treatment to save their child. Even when parents are prepared to face reality, they may bring in a newspaper article about a new drug and ask if it will help their son or daughter. We must help parents to attune their hopes to the realities of what is happening to their child.

Parents' Needs

Parents are the key to the coping pattern of the family: "As parents go, so goes the child." They are the advocates and decision makers for their children. During terminal care, parents themselves have very specific needs. At the forefront, they need emotional support in order to control their anxiety, release their anger, and temper their sadness with hope.

As caregivers, we can help parents to meet the following needs:

1. To Understand their Feelings. Parents may require assistance to understand their intense and difficult feelings. They need to know that their responses are not unusual and that each parent may not experience the same feelings at the same time. For example, the decision to stop aggressive treatment may be a relief for one parent but a destruction of hope for the other. An exploration of feelings and their meaning for each partner may help to promote understanding and tolerance as well as to reduce conflict.

2. To Release their Feelings.   Parents need to find ways to release their difficult feelings constructively. The father who has always been told to keep a "stiff upper lip," even when he was very upset, will have a difficult time expressing his feelings as he faces the death of his child. To expect him to change his approach may not be realistic. Alternative methods of expression, such as physical or artistic activities, may provide some relief to such a father.

The burden of a dying child—who is often demanding and irritable—places great stress on most marriages. The intensity of feelings arising from interpersonal conflict in a marriage may result in displaced anger, frustration, and aggression. The caregiver should, if possible, identify potential outbursts and temper them before they get out of hand.

3. To Acknowledge the Ultimate Loss of their Child.   Parents need to acknowledge the ultimate loss of their child. Coming to terms with this reality will help them to gradually work through their feelings and prepare for the final separation. Caregivers need to be objective, nonjudgmental, and willing to discuss questions about the child's impending death, the funeral, and bereavement.

4. To Understand their Religious Beliefs.   Families who have not been religiously observant may return to some form of religious practice as death approaches. A chaplain may assist those who are struggling with beliefs about a God who is apparently vengeful or arbitrary in his power. However, it is important to remember that religion may not help every family.

5. To Know Everything Possible has been Done.   Parents need to know that everything possible has been done for their child. Opportunities to speak at length with their child's physician and other caregivers may be necessary and appreciated. They need reassurance that their child is receiving the best of care and that, although death is inevitable, everything will be done to keep their child comfortable and as free from pain as possible.

6. To Help Plan for their Child's Death.   Many parents have found it helpful to make funeral arrangements prior to the time of death, when they are less upset. Caregivers can often facilitate such planning and discuss the details when relatives and friends may be unable to provide such assistance.

7. *To Participate in their Child's Care.* As caregivers, we should support and encourage parents to attend to their child's immediate needs; they should have access to their child in the hospital whenever they wish. We must acknowledge parents' needs and their right to protect their child. As death approaches, the focus of a child's life often narrows down to mother. Such an intense symbiotic bond can make a mother feel she cannot trust anyone with her child. As a result, the child clings more and more to a totally exhausted parent (Adams and Deveau 1988). We must try to temper the parents involvement so that they do not smother their child emotionally or exhaust themselves physically.

Siblings' Feelings

Cancer is a family disease; siblings do not escape the anxiety, stress, and turmoil. They are often much closer to the dying child than we may realize. They have attachments that are quite different from their relationships with adults. Spinetta (1981) has shown that siblings of children with cancer are more withdrawn, fearful, inhibited, and irritable than are siblings of children with other long-term chronic illnesses. Throughout the course of the illness, siblings may continue to have difficulty adjusting and may remain anxious because life never returns to normal for them. When their brother or sister is dying, their anxiety may be heightened and accelerated (Cairns et al. 1979). Siblings must contend with many difficult feelings when their brother or sister is dying:

Anxiety. Siblings' anxiety tends to focus on what has happened to their family and what will happen after death. When their brother's or sister's cancer is out of control they may worry that they or their parents may also get cancer and die (Sourkes 1980).

Anger. Siblings may be angry that their lives have been disrupted yet again. Their anger at the changes in family life may be directed at their parents, the physician or God. They may be angry with the adults for not protecting their sibling from dying. They may also be angry at themselves for their inability to help their dying brother or sister.

Guilt. Guilt may resurface at this time. Some siblings may feel guilty because they are angry at their brother or sister for dying. Others may feel guilty for being healthy or for saying or doing something that they believe has contributed to the return of the disease. This is especially common in 5- to 9-year-old children who believe in a cause–effect reaction. Siblings, especially adolescents, may feel guilty for not protecting their brother or sister from suffering and dying (Adams and Deveau 1987).

Jealousy.   Siblings who are close in age to, or younger than, the dying child may struggle with feelings of jealousy. It may be very difficult for them to accept the special favors, allowances, and extra time that their dying brother or sister receives from their parents and relatives.

Feeling Left Out.   As family routines change to accommodate the demands and needs of the dying child, siblings of any age may feel very much alone. Everything seems to revolve around their dying brother or sister.

> Brian, in tears one day after school, cried out to his mother: "Why does everyone keep asking me about Billy and how he is doing. . . . Nobody cares about me or ever asks anything about me or how I am doing!"

Siblings' Needs

Many of the needs of siblings parallel those of the dying child.

Love, Security, and Reassurance.   The need for love, security, and reassurance is as important to siblings as it is to the dying child.

Involvement.   One of my basic beliefs, as I mentioned earlier, is that siblings should be involved in terminal care. However, the degree of their involvement should be their decision. It is natural for parents to want to protect them from any pain and suffering, but siblings do need to be a part of the family and be allowed to participate and to share in what is happening. This will help them to work through their grief and enable them to cope better after their brother or sister has died (Lauer and Camitta 1980; Lauer, Mulhern, Bohne and Camitta 1985).

Siblings also need to be involved in living. Parents should be encouraged to continue doing routine tasks with their other children, such as taking them to hockey practices and piano lessons. They need to have their own time and their own escape. Time to be with friends and time alone provides respite as well as opportunities to sort out difficult feelings(Adams and Deveau 1987, 1988).

Honesty and Knowledge.   When we remember that siblings of children with cancer are anxious throughout the course of their brother's or sister's illness, we can understand why honesty is essential. These children must know what is happening to their brother or sister; why family routines must change; and what to expect. Such sharing and discussion will provide opportunities for these children to ask questions as well as to express their feelings.

Home Care

In the preceding pages I have identified and examined the feelings and needs of dying children and family members. Let us now consider how we plan for terminal care, keeping in mind the issues and dilemmas addressed at the beginning.

A review of the literature suggests that death at home may be preferable to death in the hospital. Martinson (1979) notes that dying children under age 14 universally preferred to die at home. If parents can accept the fact that their child is dying, and trust their own ability to provide care, then home care is beneficial and may temper their anxiety and sadness. Mulhern, Lauer, and Hoffman (1983) note that parents who participate in home care programs are less anxious, depressed, and defensive. In a follow-up study one year after the death of a brother or sister at home, Lauer and her associates (1985) found that siblings believed that they had:

- Received more consistent information and support from parents;
- Viewed their own involvement as the most important part of their experience; and
- Felt capable of handling what had transpired.

Their experiences were diametrically opposite to those of siblings whose brother or sister had died in the hospital.

Special Requirements of Home Care

Before home care can be implemented, the dying child's pain must be under control. Twenty-four-hour medical support and an open-door policy at the hospital should be established. Parents must have the option to bring their child back to the hospital at any time without feeling guilty or believing that they have failed. Can emergency room staff be alerted? Can a "no code" order be written in advance? Can admissions be streamlined?

When possible, the following advance arrangements should also be in place:

- An ambulance, ready to respond as necessary;
- Contact with a funeral home, with tentative preparations made;
- Explanation and discussion with the parents regarding a request from the child's physician for an autopsy.

Home Care Versus Hospital Care

Before examining the benefits and outcomes of home care vs. hospital care for the dying child and family members, I wish to acknowledge the pioneering work of Ida Martinson and her colleagues.

The Dying Child.   Table 1-1 demonstrates that care at home provides greater flexibility and less need for regimented routines than does care in the hospital.

In the relaxed surroundings of the home, dying children tend to be more alert and often require less medication. Parents are able to use their own judgement and have greater control over nursing measures, including the management of pain (Martinson 1978).

Children at home are usually less isolated and lonely. Friends may visit, children may have access to their backyards, and pets are nearby. Home usually means that the family can remain together and support each other rather than be divided, with one parent away at the hospital (Martinson 1978; Mount and McHarg 1987).

Table 1-1.
Benefits of Home Care: The Child

Hospital Care	Home Care
Nursing and Medical Care	
–Parents have less control	–Parents have more control
–Routine-oriented	–More flexible
Pain Control	
–Depends on regimens	–More flexible
–Unfamiliar surroundings	–Relaxed surroundings
–More anxiety—increased medication	–More alert—decreased medication
–Depends on judgement and availability of staff	–Dependent on parental judgement
Isolation and Loneliness	
–Restricted by hospital routines	–Not restricted by routines
–Away from familiar surroundings	–In familiar surroundings
–Limited access to peers	–Easier access to peers
Family Dynamics	
Communication	
–May be inhibited	–More opportunities
–Limited access to family except mother	–Easier access to whole family
Togetherness	
–Family often divided	–Family together
–Strain on individual members	–More sharing and support
Sibling Involvement	
–Less involved	–More involved
–More difficult to visit	–More available

Parents.   Table 1-2 outlines the benefits of home care for parents. At home, parents have unlimited access to their child, with opportunities for support and assistance from extended family. Since they retain full responsibility for their child's care, they can ensure that important needs, such as rest and privacy, are met (Martinson 1978; Adams 1979; Adams and Deveau 1984, 1988).

Fewer expenses may be accrued at home because there is less need for travel to the treatment center, accommodation and meals away from home, and babysitting (Lauer and Camitta 1980).

Follow-up studies indicate that when children died at home, family members felt less guilty because they believed they had done everything possible (Martinson 1978). In addition, there were fewer instances of interpersonal problems in these families (Mulhern, Lauer, and Hoffman 1983).

Table 1-2.
Benefits of Home Care: Parents

Hospital Care	Home Care
Time with Dying Child	
–More difficult (e.g., distance, hospital policies)	–More opportunity (24-hour availability)
Shared Workload	
–Difficult	–Easier
–Wife often absent from home	–Extended family more available
	–Family members usually present
–Limited by hospital policies	–More flexibility
Dying Child's Care	
–Policies dictate care	–Parents control care
–Limited control over environment	–Control over physical environment (e.g., rest, privacy)
–Parents protect child from limited care	–Parents have full responsibility for care
Emotional Support for Parents	
–Limited access to family and friends	–Easier access to family and friends
Financial Burdens	
–Increased expenses (e.g., travel, food)	–Fewer expenses at home
Adjustment After Death	
–Family less likely to be together	–Family shares dying process
–More guilt (Could we have done more?)	–Less guilt (We did everything possible)
–More depression and interpersonal problems	–Less depression and fewer interpersonal problems

Siblings. In Table 1-3, it is evident that home care provides siblings with easier access to their dying brother or sister. There are also greater opportunities for them to obtain information, be involved in discussions, and participate in the care of the dying child. Parents are nearby to provide emotional support, and these children are more likely to be present at the time of death.

As noted earlier, siblings whose brother or sister died at home were better prepared for the death and felt less guilty than when the death occurred in the hospital (Lauer, Mulhern, Bohne, and Camitta 1985).

Table 1-3.
Benefits of Home Care: Siblings

Hospital Care	Home Care
Knowledge re: Disease and Dying	
–Easily excluded	–More apt to be included
–Limited access to information	–Easier access to information
–Limited access to child and parents	–Easier access to child and parents
Involvement	
–Access difficult, e.g., distance	–Access easier → more involvement
–Feel useless, not active in care	–Feel appreciated
–Less likely to be present at death	–Usually present at death
Parent Support for Siblings	
–More difficult	–More accessible
Anxiety	
–Unfamiliar surroundings	–Familiar surroundings
–Restricted access to child	–Open access
–Parental absence from home	–Parents present
Adjustment After Death	
–Feel inadequately prepared for death	–Feel better prepared for death
–Less involved → more guilt	–More involved → less guilt
–Feel they could have done more	–Feel everything possible done

Possible Negative Outcomes of Home Care

Although I have outlined many benefits provided by home care for the dying child, parents, and siblings, there are certain disadvantages, as indicated in Table 1-4. For example, prearrangements for the establishment of home care may be difficult and frustrating. Greater demands are placed on these families as they assume full responsibility at home. The most difficult task arises from coping with the child's pain and suffering. This is especially taxing if access to professional support is limited. If complications arise and the child must return to the hospital, parents may believe that they have failed and feel guilty.

At home, parents may also be isolated from contact with other parents. Some may be burdened with relatives and other adults who may be critical because they believe that the hospital is "the best place to die." On the other hand, the hospital provides continuous management of medical problems. Professionals are more readily available for support and guidance during the dying process, and hospital staff assume full responsibility for any complications (Martinson 1978).

It has been suggested that the hospital offers protection for parents from pain and suffering. When professionals assume responsibility for complications, then parents have fewer reasons to feel guilty (Martinson 1978). Like Martinson, I believe that this viewpoint is debatable.

Table 1-4.
Possible Negative Outcomes of Home Care

Hospital Care	Home Care
Social Acceptability	
–Hospital viewed as "best place to die"	–Adults and relatives may criticize death at home
Emotional Strain	
–Access to professional support easier –Support available from other parents –Protected from dying process	–Access to professional support difficult –Isolated from other parents –Deal directly with child's pain and suffering
Parental Responsibility re: Dying Child's Care	
–Professionals assume responsibility –Fewer opportunities for parental guilt	–Parents assume responsibility –May feel guilty for complications, failure to manage at home
Medical Care	
–Close at hand	–Must be prearranged –Arrangements may be difficult
Physical Demands on Family	
–Fewer demands –Family is auxiliary to staff	–More demands –Intense involvement
Anxiety re: Death	
–Management of medical problems by professionals	–Constant fear of medical problems

| –Professionals available during dying process | –Professionals may not be available during dying process |

Conclusion

It is true that we cannot always predict when a child is dying. However, in most cases, terminal care can be planned, but only if professionals and families work together so that everyone understands that (a) death will occur; (b) differences must be aired; (c) compromises must be reached; and (d) areas of responsibility must be delineated clearly so that everyone truly acts in the best interest of the child.

Care should be continuous. There must be sharing between the pediatric oncology team and those who provide home care. The family's desire for linkage and dialogue with those who have been close to the child should be maintained. Community caregivers must be given sanction, legitimacy, and support through the pediatric oncology team.

Children have a right to be comforted, to be children, and to make choices. As caregivers, we can help to reduce their suffering, to temper rules, and to involve them in decision making. Unfortunately, we must recognize that there will be times when children's wishes and needs may be only partially met because of family and/or medical problems and limitations.

Dying is a family concern. We need to encourage parents to involve their other children throughout the course of the illness. When appropriate, these children need to be included in discussions, decision making, and actual care of their dying brother or sister. Their degree of involvement should be determined by their age and abilities as well as personal choice. Parents may need help to avoid overburdening adolescents or overprotecting younger children.

I believe that death is best at home in familiar surroundings with family present. However, I recognize that this is not realistic and feasible for every family. Caregivers must try to meet the needs of dying children and their families, given their particular circumstances. We should be flexible enough to facilitate at least some time at home with adequate support and services in place.

References

Adams, D. W. 1979. *Childhood malignancy: The psychosocial care of the child and his family.* Springfield, IL: C. C. Thomas.

———1984. Helping the dying child: Practical approaches for non- physicians. In H. Wass and C. A. Corr, eds. *Childhood and Death.* Washington, DC: Hemisphere Publishing, pp. 95–112.

Adams, D. W. and E. J. Deveau. 1988. *Coping with childhood cancer: Where do we go from here?* rev. ed. Hamilton, Ontario: Kinbridge Publications. (1st ed.: Reston, VA: Reston Publishing Co., 1984.)

———1987. When a brother or sister is dying of cancer: The vulnerability of the adolescent sibling. *Death Studies* 11:279–95.

Cairns, N. U., G. M. Clark, S. D. Smith and S. B. Lansky. 1979. Adaptation of siblings to childhood malignancy. *Journal of Pediatrics* 95:484–87.

Chesler, M. A. and O. A. Barbarin. 1987. *Childhood cancer and the family.* New York: Brunner/ Mazel.

Corr, C. A. and D. M. Corr. 1985. Pediatric hospice care. *Pediatrics* 76(5): 774–80. Also see Corr, C. A. and D. M. Corr, 1985. *Hospice approaches to pediatric care.* New York: Springer.

Greenberg, M. 1988. A dream shatters—A child is dying. Paper presented at conference A Child is Dying, Mohawk College, May 18, Hamilton, Ontario.

Hamovitch, M. B. 1964. *The parent and the fatally ill child.* Duarte, CA: City of Hope Medical Center.

Lauer, M. and B. Camitta. 1980. Home care for dying children: A nursing model. *Journal of Pediatrics* 97:1032–35.

Lauer, M., R. Mulhearn, J. Bohne and B. Camitta. 1985. Children's perceptions of their sibling's death at home or hospital: The precursors of differential adjustment. *Cancer Nursing* February: 21–27.

Martinson, I. M. 1978. Alternative environments for the care of the dying child: Hospice, hospitals or home. In O. J. Sahler, ed. *The child and death.* St. Louis, MO: C. V. Mosby, pp. 83–91.

———1979. Home care for the child with cancer. *Care of the child with cancer.* New York: American Cancer Society, pp. 163–66. Also see Martinson, I. M., ed. (1976). *Home care for the dying child: Professional and family perspectives.* New York: Appleton-Century-Crofts.

Mount, B. M. and L. F. McHarg. 1987. *The Montreal children's palliative care assessment committee report.* Montreal: pp. 126–39.

Mulhern, R., M. Lauer and R. Hoffman. 1983. Death of a child at home or in the hospital: Subsequent psychological adjustment of the family. *Pediatrics* 71:743–47.

Sourkes, B. 1980. Siblings of the pediatric cancer patient. In J. Kellerman, ed. *Psychological aspects of childhood cancer.* Springfield, IL: C. C. Thomas.

Spinetta, J. J. 1977. Communication patterns in families of children with life threatening illness. Paper presented at postgraduate symposium, The Child and Death, University of Rochester, Rochester, New York.

———1978. Communication patterns in families dealing with life threatening illness. In O. J. Sahler, ed. *The child and death.* St. Louis, MO: C. V. Mosby, pp. 43–46.

———1981. The siblings of the child with cancer. In Spinetta and P. Deasy-Spinetta, eds. *Living with childhood cancer.* St. Louis, MO: C. V. Mosby, pp. 137–40.

2

The Role of the Professional in an Adolescent Support Group for those with Cancer

Kathryn Hustins, RN, PhD and Colleen Kelly, RN, PhD

Adolescence is a time of elation and depression, hyperactivity and lethargy, verbosity and muteness, happiness and pain. It is above all a developmental period greatly characterized by change. It is the very nature of this change that makes working with adolescents such an exciting and challenging experience.

The adolescent usually perceives herself as invincible. Death is seen as something far in the unforeseeable future. And because most people continue to associate the diagnosis of cancer with death, the adolescent who has cancer and who seems so full of life often unwittingly creates stress, anger, and sadness in family and friends.

Most adolescents with cancer cope extremely well. The adolescent has the resiliency to spring back and function in spite of adverse situations. Often it appears that the limited expectations of others may be more disabling to the adolescent than the disease itself. However, research indicates that some adolescents with cancer have significant psychosocial problems. Not only do they have to deal with the disruption to the developmental tasks of adolescence, but they must also contend with the uncertainty of a life-threatening illness. Given the complexity of the problems that confront adolescents, it is not surprising that studies of adolescents with cancer reveal alarming rates of noncompliance, behavioral problems, severe anxiety, and clinical depression (Kashami and Hakami 1982) as well as school phobia (Lansky et al. 1976), and peer rejection (Carr-Gregg 1986).

A survey of services available to adolescents and their families in Newfoundland indicates that those services tend to be very diverse and fragmented. Many adolescents receive their treatment in adult and pediatric oncology units. They

22

are rarely afforded the opportunity to interact with similarly affected peers or with staff members who are trained specifically in working with this age group. Consequently, their requirements for information are not always met, especially with respect to the side-effects of treatment, the likelihood of a recurrence, how to deal with the social isolation and stigmatization, the effects on their sexuality and long term prognosis (Carr-Gregg and Hampson 1986). Adolescents' needs for privacy, some degree of participation in their treatment, appropriate recreational opportunities to discuss and understand the nature of their physical problems, and an ability to maintain contact with peers and family, have all been identified as issues that need to be resolved. Many adolescents with cancer feel isolated from their family, their peers, and their community (Carr-Gregg and Hampson 1986). They confess to living with fear of relapse and often have no one with whom they feel able to share their anxieties and fears (Carr-Gregg 1986).

Today 50 percent of people diagnosed with cancer will be alive five years after diagnosis (Ziegfield 1987). Goldberg and Tull (1983) state that cancer remains the most common life-threatening illness of adolescents. Medical advances, however, have significantly increased the survival rate for many childhood cancers (Jamison, Lewis, and Burish 1986). Cancer has become a chronic illness associated with exacerbations and remissions (Holing 1986). Many survivors of childhood cancer reach adulthood, marry, have children, and participate as active members of society (Teta 1986).

An increasingly effective form of psychosocial intervention that is currently being used to facilitate adjustment and coping is that of oncology patient support groups (Heiney et al. 1984), parent support groups (Heffron et al. 1973; Gilder et al. 1978), and groups for the siblings of patients with cancer (Cunningham et al. 1981). Let us now look at the development of an organization that is concerned with adolescents with cancer in Newfoundland—Candles for Hope.

In discussing the development of Candles for Hope, this chapter focuses on the evolving role of the professional in the establishment of an adolescent support group during the first year. The role will be explored through two important factors that strongly affect the growth and development of the adolescent: 1) how adolescents best learn, and 2) concerns adolescents express that arise in the activity of daily living. These important factors will influence the supportive role of the professional as well as determine the involvement of the adolescent. Before exploring these factors in detail, it is important to have an appreciation of exactly what problems confront the adolescent.

Coping with Cancer

Adolescence is a particularly difficult growth period in which to deal with a cancer diagnosis and treatment. It is during adolescence that achieving independence and determining one's identity are primary aspects of growth and development. The cancer diagnosis and treatment often increase feelings of helplessness, a sense of loss of control over one's body right down to the cellular level, and loss of control within self over the outcome of the situation. Seligman (1973, 1974) believed an individual could learn helplessness. Those who had a sense of learned helplessness were poorly motivated and had impaired cognitive function. The future was perceived as bleak, control over pleasure was lost, and a sense of powerlessness prevailed. The adolescent who is protected during illness and hospitalization, who is not encouraged to be independent or participate in choice of treatment, and not given the opportunity to express feelings, is more likely to develop feelings of learned helplessness and powerlessness.

Personality integration and coping skills required for dealing with the cancer experience are not well developed in the adolescent (Snyder 1986). Adolescents do have the cognitive ability to comprehend matters of diagnosis, treatment, and prognosis. Coping strategies or methods used to promote resolution of, or control over, a threatening situation where one feels helplessness can be learned. Adolescence is the key period for developing effective coping strategies for a lifetime. If successful, the adolescent is more likely to fulfill the growth tasks of adolescence related to issues of independence and self-identity. These tasks can be met even though one lives with the chronic and life-threatening nature of cancer.

Goldberg and Tull (1983) believed coping could be assisted by providing information, and encouraging independence and self-care. These authors believed the adolescent may have a greater capacity to cope than does the adult faced with threatening experiences. They attributed this mainly to the common adolescent characteristics of honest straightforwardness and a confrontative personality. Acceptance of questioning and of honest responses increase the adolescent's sense of trust in the adult. This in itself promotes a sense of power over threatening situations.

Jameson et al. (1986) identified studies supporting the theory that the adolescent's self-esteem is lowered due to the chronic nature of cancer, and that adolescent cancer patients have a lower internal locus of control than do healthy peers. Adolescents in remission perceived themselves as well and had strong coping mechanisms. The research also showed adolescents with cancer had an external locus-of-control orientation in powerful others. This was not perceived as negative, but as a beneficial means of reducing stress related to loss of internal locus of control. This reinforces the belief in the feelings of powerlessness associated with chronic illness.

Many of the threatening situations the adolescent is forced to cope with during acute and chronic periods of the cancer experience are primarily associated with loss. These losses are reflected in the following concerns most frequently expressed by the adolescent living with cancer:

1. lowered self-esteem
2. altered body image
3. forced dependency
4. isolation from peers
5. confusion and anxiety about future outcomes and illnesses
6. fear of potential treatment interventions in the future
7. interference with education
8. questioning hopes for marriage and children (Goldberg and Tull 1983)

These are discussed in more detail in the section "Concerns Expressed by Adolescents in a Support Group."

Peer Influence and Peer Support

Erikson's theory (1963) of ego identity versus ego confusion is clearly identified with adolescent growth and development. According to Erikson, the adolescent seeks answers to "Who am I" and "What am I to be." The psychosocial task of the adolescent is the establishment of identity. The danger of this stage is that of role confusion. In each of Erikson's developmental stages, the individual must make a choice and come to terms with the outcome. The choice involves both positive and negative aspects, depending on whether the "crisis" has been successfully resolved.

Recent studies indicate that the optimum time for teaching adolescents appears to be between grades seven through twelve (Stiles 1980). From puberty onward there is an increasing emphasis on peer approval. Adolescence is a time of growing abstract conceptualization in that idealism and fighting for causes is common. To be outside this group is to be "odd."

Identification with a peer group may be so powerful that the adolescent may temporarily lose his sense of identity. Kohlberg (1975) believed that peer relationships are a more positive influence on an adolescent's socialization than the influence of a parent.

The use of positive peer influence has become increasingly popular in the educational setting as well as in the health care environment. Health education has long utilized peer influence when dealing with problems such as substance abuse, eating disorders, and weight control (Edmund 1986), as well as other high- risk areas of adolescent health and development. Peer interaction is used for positive outcome through peer support groups. In peer education, a valuable and important learning experience is often the spontaneous and informal interaction that occurs when two adolescents exchange ideas and information.

The defining force of the individual's progression toward adulthood is the opportunity to be competent, to be responsible for themselves, to seize and utilize available resources, and to meet personal and familial challenges. As Letton (1977) suggests,

> It is our duty not to simply heal the tumor but to heal the whole person-make him live a useful and productive life no matter how short or how long it can be. What does it profiteth (*sic*) a man to cure him of cancer if he lose his ability to live? (p.24)

To "win through" an experience of cancer, the individual must have resources available to alleviate long-term stress and to reinforce efficacy and confidence.

Peer support groups are not counseling or therapy groups. They are, rather, experiential groups using common experiences in order for members to educate each other for life (Monaco 1986). This is an important distinction for professionals to keep in mind. Peer groups are not doing the professional's job and therefore should not be considered a threat. The adolescent often best learns from peer-to-peer contact. Support groups offer a mechanism whereby adolescents can explore, share, and discuss concerns and experiences. A nurturing, supportive environment can enhance the development of effective coping strategies, enhance growth and development, and promote completion of developmental tasks.

Although each group is unique in its membership, focus, and activities, all self-help groups can serve as potent tools in combating anxiety, fright, pain, loneliness, and anger (Pinkel 1978). These groups often instruct members in methods of dealing with practical problems. Many former cancer patients have found that helping others also boosts their own self-esteem, and individuals often benefit from the opportunities to aid others faced with the same crisis (Hartman 1980).

In most groups, health professionals are actively involved and valued as a source of support and encouragement, as long as they refrain from trying to "run" the group or exercise direct leadership. The groups with professionals who offer counseling, facilitating, training, and intervention where needed, also appear to thrive. This shared leadership concept seems to allow for the highest rate of individual participation. It also presents an excellent arena for active coping and for working out an innovative form of partnership with health care professionals (Yoak et al. 1983).

Among the advantages of an adolescent peer support group is that of providing adolescents with cancer a milieu in which they can tackle the tasks of adolescence while adjusting to life with cancer. Such a group encourages open communication about cancer, its treatment, side-effects and prognosis (Yoak et al. 1983). It conveys the message that it is permissible to express fears and anxieties. Common concerns of many adolescents with cancer, such as overprotection by parents and others, changes in physical appearance, loss of control, feelings of guilt, and the difficulties in living a "normal" life tend to be discussed in an informal, nonthreatening fashion, with the more experienced adolescents helping those who have been recently diagnosed.

This structure also provides a transitional peer group, giving the adolescent with cancer whose communication and social skills have been affected negatively by his illness an opportunity to rejoin the mainstream of adolescent life, thereby helping to alleviate his sense of isolation. The group allows adolescents who have survived treatment to feel that they can make a contribution in return, by assisting others in the same predicament. Some research suggests that the therapeutic value of such interactions is substantial (Mogtader 1986).

The Development of Candles for Hope

Candles for Hope came into being when nurses in an acute-care adult hospital observed that the needs of both in- and outpatient adolescents dealing with cancer were different from those of adult cancer patients. Nurses often felt stressed and helpless caring for adolescent patients when treatment and follow-up problems occurred. Adolescents who attended a provincial summer camp and who had been treated at the children's hospital expressed a desire to meet more frequently, discuss concerns, and receive support.

Having recognized the need, both of us decided to organize a support group to meet the needs of adolescents with cancer between ages 14 to 21. Because of the independent nature of the adolescent, it was decided that the role of the professional was to function primarily as a facilitator. The structure, aims, and activities of the group would be determined by the adolescents themselves, who could best determine their own needs.

During the early meetings the adolescents present were from 17 to 19 years of age. They agreed that the aim of the group was to be supportive only. It was open to any adolescent from 14 to 21 years of age who was coping with cancer. Registration was not required. There were no rules except that of confidentiality and a willingness to share. The adolescents were free to attend as they wished. The group agreed to meet every two weeks on Saturday afternoon from 2 to 4 o'clock. The adolescents requested that the meeting place be away from an area where peers would be able to see them. This, they felt, would avoid the risk of being singled out as different, best reflected in the statement: "The other kids won't understand."

Initial meetings focused on suggested activities. These included networking with other adolescents in isolated parts of the province via teleconference, fund-raising, developing a provincial newsletter, and identifying activities for educating teachers and students about the cancer experience. The adolescents identified topics they wanted to discuss. These included body image, chemotherapy, steroid treatments, hair loss, and stress reduction. At later meetings, the group suggested making a video of their cancer experience for the education of their peers, teachers, and others.

Several difficulties were encountered during the past year. The group was slow in getting started, which affected motivation and enthusiasm. Some adolescents would not come, believing that the group was one of "spilling your guts, crying, and all that stuff." For some there were distance obstacles up to 80 miles (50 km). During the maritime Canadian winter this posed a major problem. The adolescents who attended were those who were treated in the pediatric setting. Response from the adult setting was not successful for reasons of distance or conflict with treatment plans. It should be noted that males did not attend these meetings. It was questioned whether the absence of a male facilitator may have played a part in this lack of participation. Another difficulty encountered was that of informing and explaining to others our desire for independence as a group, and our nonaffiliation or association with an established organization or institution. It was felt that by being independent the adolescents would have a group of their own where they could learn to be self-directed in discovering ways to meet their particular needs and could feel a sense of collective pride in addressing and conquering some of their concerns.

Overall, we believe that Candles for Hope has been very successful in providing an arena for the growth and development of the adolescent with cancer. The participants had the opportunity to express those concerns most relevant to them at this time in their lives.

Concerns Expressed by the Adolescents in Their Support Group

Interference with education long after treatments were completed was a concern frequently expressed. Some adolescents had to deal only with problems of missing time and keeping up with their friends and classmates. Others had to deal with actual changes in learning ability resulting from the effects of neurosurgery, cranial radiation, and intrathecal chemotherapy. Facing the reality of not being able to reach the same scholastic level as before the cancer experience and dealing with the expectations of others based on past performance can be difficult. For many, being treated differently from classmates by teachers worsened the situation. Preferential treatment for assignments, homework, projects, and tests only reinforced feelings of helplessness, being different, and subsequently affected self-esteem. The university environment also posed problems resulting from anonymity and self- responsibility as an adult learner. Being lost in the crowd compared to being part of a crowd as in high school precipitated feelings of helplessness not uncommon to many adolescents in their early months of secondary education. For some, this arena is where they may first learn that others are not interested in making exceptions based on past life experiences.

Forced dependency is often reflected in the literature in overprotectiveness by parents. Simple trips to the physician can be embarrassing for those who feel very capable of making this journey alone, but find a parent wanting to be there as well. The adolescent's need for greater autonomy and privacy is sometimes overlooked. Often the adolescent must act according to the rules the parent sets for good behavior in such situations. A sense of powerlessness arises and feelings of helplessness surface. Parents often have difficulty in allowing independence in such areas as career choices, taking trips away from home, moving to further education, and selecting social activities with peers. The health care system often serves to reinforce this sense of forced dependency and helplessness. Adolescents may learn through sharing their feelings, but this may not be enough to overcome the feelings of dependency. The adolescent will need social skills aimed at increasing self-reliance and creating an internal locus of control without consequent guilt and difficulties with parents. The group offers an arena for finding resources for self-development—for example, assertiveness training. It also offers encouragement to be open and honest with adults in expressing desires, needs, and, more important, feelings. As facilitators we have found it helpful to share our own feelings of situational powerlessness and how we have coped with them. We revealed our failures, discussed the process of growth that followed them, and told how we had conquered similar problems.

Years after treatment completion, changes in body image are constant reminders to the adolescent of the cancer experience and of their perception of being different. Alopecia, a reversible condition for most, is especially traumatic for the female for whom it is irreversible. Wigs commonly look like wigs and nonverbal expressions of others confirm this. An amputation often elicits the question "How did you lose your leg?" Bloating from prednisone, coordination difficulties caused by nerve and muscle damage from treatment, and speech difficulty, are only a few of the handicaps that can remind others of "being different." The adolescent who is very sensitive and self-conscious of body changes and the reactions of others, will tend to avoid socializing with peers. It is during socialization that the adolescent matures emotionally, gains a sense of identity, develops relationships with others, begins dating, and determines a direction for the future. Adolescents appear to have little difficulty speaking with others who have cancer and with others they trust of their personal growth through the cancer experience. In the group, embarrassing situations were often shared in a humorous and lighthearted way and in an accepting and trusting environment. Outside the group, perceptions of being different are more difficult to deal with, without skills to help cope with feelings of inferiority, helplessness, and decreased self-esteem. As one of the members of the group expressed quite emphatically: "After having cancer one feels very vulnerable in the face of the world. It is very difficult to get back those feelings of confidence and well-being when relating to others.''

Uncertainty of the future because of illness came to the forefront when the group acknowledged briefly the death of a friend with cancer and the recent hospitalization of another friend who had gone several years without any recurrence of cancer. From our perspective, it appeared that the adolescents recognized the death of the friend and the possible exacerbation of another friend's cancer, but they did not express any desire to discuss these events. One member of the group found a creative way to express the grief of the group in her poetry—a poem she chose to display to the public at the annual Health Fair Day.

Marriage and having children appeared to be concerns of the distant future for the girls in the group. Most were at the point of addressing issues related to dating. Whereas interest in boys was discussed, the girls stated that because of their experience, they were more mature than most boys their age and were different emotionally because of the experience. They did indicate the desire to marry and have children someday, but having a career was a more immediate priority.

Fears regarding possible treatment interventions in the future (a concern noted in the literature) were not expressed within the group. Isolation from peers appeared to be a major concern during hospitalization and subsequent early years of survival.

Some of the most productive interactions of the group occurred during outings and craft activities. On occasion the adolescents chose recorded music that served to enhance the mood. It was interesting that most of the music spanned the generations between us: music of the Beatles, the Beach Boys, Simon and Garfunkel. During the craft activities, issues related to sexuality were brought up by the adolescents, including menstruation, sexual intercourse, and birth control. In retrospect, we noted that the adolescents could choose to make or not to make eye contact during these sessions by virtue of needing to keep their eyes on the craft objects they were making. This may have actually promoted discussion, as they did not have to respond to the nonverbal communication of others. Completing projects enhanced the adolescents' self-esteem. The Health Fair Project was especially beneficial in promoting self-esteem as participants learned how to present themselves to the community and receive responses from others. They were expected to interact with visitors to the booth and had us as role models when necessary. During the fair, particular talents of individuals came through—for example, creativity in designing a poster and the ability to create in a poem the feelings aroused by the loss of a friend through death.

The group has made many plans for future projects: a dance in the fall, making a video for teaching others, open meetings for invited friends and relatives, and publication of a newsletter. They wish to correspond with others who have a group similar to theirs or with adolescents who are planning to organize a similar group.

Conclusion

As professionals in Candles for Hope, we share our experiences, which in turn stimulates participation. The adolescents see the group as their responsibility, organizing activities and taking claim for successes and failures. Professionals take responsibility within such a group by providing a therapeutic milieu in which there is sharing, experiencing and feeling situations of happiness and pain. We have grown personally as well as professionally as we learn from these adolescents who have a wisdom and maturity far beyond their years. Our approach to the adolescent with cancer in Candles for Hope is "What are you going to do with the here and now, and how can we support and help you?"

With advances in medical treatment and care, a shift has evolved from a focus on dying to a focus on living. It is time to move to encourage the adolescent to assume responsibility for his or her own future. We are not suggesting that we discontinue the many support programs that are in place, but that we put the adolescent at the center of his or her own destiny. We must provide adolescents with information and knowledge, understanding, support and guidance as they learn to cope with the daily and long-term demands of living with a diagnosis of cancer. Let us help them but not as professional-to-client, not as superior-to-inferior, and not as adult-to-child, but as equal partners in life's struggles (Spinetta and Deasy-Spinetta 1986). The reward for our efforts as professionals will be an adolescent who will in the long run be empowered and strengthened to be one day a productive, contributing member of society.

References

Battista, E. 1986. Emotional needs of the adolescent with cancer and his family. *Seminars in Oncology Nursing* 2(2):123–25.

Bellinger, B. 1986. Growing up differently: an adolescents perspective. *Seminars in Oncology Nursing* 2(2):84–89.

Blotcky, A. 1986. Helping adolescents with cancer cope with their disease. *Seminars in Oncology Nursing* 2(2):117–22.

Brown, M. et al. 1986. *Standards of oncology nursing practice.* New York: John Wiley and Sons.

Carr-Gregg, M.R.C. 1986. The adolescent with cancer in Australia. *Australian Association Adolescent Health Newsletter* 26:29–33.

Carr-Gregg, M.R.C. and R. Hampson. 1986. A new approach to the psychological care of adolescents with cancer. *The Medical Journal of Australia* 1(5):580–83.

Cunningham, C., N. Betsa and S. Gross. 1981. Sibling groups—interactions with siblings of oncology patients. *American Journal of American Pediatric Oncology* 3:135–39.

Edmund, M. 1986. Overcoming eating disorders—a group experience. *Journal of Psychosocial Nursing* 24(8):19–25.

Erikson, E.H. 1963. *Childhood and society.* 2nd ed. New York: W.W. Norton.

Gilder, R., R. R. Buschmsan, A. L. Sitarz and J. A. Wolf. 1978. Group therapy with parents of children with leukemia. *American Journal of Psychotherapy* 32:276–87.

Goldberg, R. and M. Tull. 1983. *The psychosocial dimensions of cancer.* New York: The Free Press.

Hartman, J. B. 1980. *Taking time.* Bethesda, MD: National Cancer Institute.

Heffron, W. A., K. Bommelaere and R. Masters. 1973. Group discussions with parents of leukemia children. *Pediatrics* 52:831–40.

Heiney, S. P., J. Ruffin, R. Ettinger, et al. 1984. The effects of group therapy on adolescents with cancer. *Journal of the Association of Pediatric Nursing* 1:16–17.

Holing, E. 1986. The primary caregiver's perception of the dying trajectory. *Cancer Nursing* 9(11):29–37.

Jameson, R.N., S. Lewis and T. Burish. 1986. Psychological impact of cancer on adolescents: Self-image, locus of control, perception of illness and knowledge of cancer. *Journal of Chronic Diseases* 39(8):609–17.

Kashani, J. and D. Hakami. 1982. Depression in children and adolescents with malignancy. *Canadian Journal of Psychiatry* 27:474–77.

Kohlberg, L. 1971. *Recent research in moral development.* New York: Holt, Rinehart and Winston.

Langsky, S.B., J.T. Lowman, T. Vats and J. Gyulay. 1976. School phobia in children with malignant neoplasms. *American Journal of Disabled Children* 129:42–46.

Letton, A. 1977. The person with cancer in the community. In *Proceedings of the American cancer society second national conference on human values and cancer.* New York: American Cancer Society.

Mogtader, E. M. and P. T. Leff. 1986. Young healers: Chronically ill adolescents as child life assistants. *Child Health Care* 14:174–77.

Monaco, G. P. 1986. Resources available to the family of child with cancer. *Cancer* 58:516–21.

Pinkel, D. 1978. Cure of the child with cancer: Definition and prospective. In *Proceedings of the national conference on the care of the child with cancer.* New York: American Cancer Society.

Seligman, M. 1973. Fall into Helplessness. *Psychology Today*, 7(1), 43–47.

———1974. Submissive Death: Giving Up on Life. *Psychology Today*, 8(5), 80–85.

Snyder, B. C. 1986. *Oncology nursing.* Boston: Little, Brown.

Spinetta, J. J. and P. Deasy-Spinetta. 1986. The patient's socialization in the community and school during therapy. *Cancer* 58:512–15.

Stiles, D. 1970. Leadership training for high school girls: An intervention at one school. *Journal of Counselling* 65(4):211–12.

Teta, M. J. et al. 1986. Psychosocial consequences of childhood and adolescent cancer survival. *Journal of Chronic Diseases* 39(9):751–59.

Yoak, M., B. K. Chesney and N. H. Schwartz. 1983. *Active roles in self-help groups for parents of children with cancer.* Ann Arbor: University of Michigan Center for Research on Social Organization.

Zeltzer, L. K. 1980. The adolescent with cancer. In Jonathan Kellerman, ed. *Psychological aspects of childhood cancer.* Springfield, IL: Charles C. Thomas.

Ziegfeld, C. 1987. *Core curriculum for oncology nursing.* Philadelphia: W. B. Saunders Company.

Part II
The Bereaved Teenager

3

Who Am I Now?
A Sibling Shares Her Grief

Alicia M. Sims

When I was four, my brother Austin Van died of a malignant brain tumor. He was 13 months old and I loved him more than anything. I loved being a big sister and taking care of him.

We called him Big A because he was so small, but he fought so hard to live that he must have been part giant! I used to hold him and snuggle in my Mom's big rocking chair and Austin always had a smile for me. We talked a lot and I shared my secrets with him.

My brother was so special to us that we called him the Rainbow Man. Even when he was so terribly sick he smiled for me, like a rainbow peeking around the dark clouds. I could always get him to grin and when he smiled, I wasn't so scared.

My Mom and Dad call me their Sunshine. We laugh and joke a lot. We did when Austin was alive, too. But right after he died, it was pretty dark for a while. It seemed like we would never be happy again. After he died, I didn't know if I was still a sister. I really didn't know who I was. Everything was topsy-turvey for a long time. I just didn't know what was happening.

When my brother died, I didn't know what dead was. I thought he was at the hospital. I was mad at my parents because they said that I couldn't see him anymore. I cried because they were crying. I was confused and alone. None of my friends would talk to me about him and they all seemed to cringe at Austin's name. He was still a part of the family, wasn't he?

My family chose to learn from his death. We realized that there was nothing we could do to change or prevent the things that had happened to us, but we did have the power to learn from them.

I want to share with you some of the things that we learned.

Many adults do not even recognize that children experience grief. Society tends to pacify itself with the rationale that "children are resilient" and that we "bounce back." However, we are not rubber balls, and we need as much compassion and concerned support as adults do in adapting to dramatic or traumatic changes.

Every child will experience the death of someone or something they love. Yet we are often shuttled off or ignored by grieving adults who may not have the energy, resources, or understanding necessary to help. By the time we are five, we know that squashed bugs make mothers sick, that belly-up goldfish get "flushed," and that everyone must whisper when someone dies. (I don't know why we have to whisper . . . I wonder who is sleeping?)

As children we have an awareness of death even if we don't talk a lot about it. Television, comics, books, and conversations overheard all help us in forming ideas. Our ideas about death and loss change with age, development, and experience. As experience with death grows, from observing the death of flowers, insects, and birds to that of pets and people, our concepts of death widen.

One of the many problems in dealing with children and death is the tendency of adults to equate their own perceptions of death with those of the child. But children are not simply little adults. We are people, each of us unique, and constantly striving to make sense of our world.

I would like to share with you some commonly recognized developmental stages of understanding about death. This information comes from research conducted by Nagy and Feifel. This is not a rigid schema, but rather gives us a general idea about how children interpret death at various stages in their lives.

Ages 3 to 5   —Temporary, capable of returning (grandma on trip)
              —Not universal (old people only)
              —Enfeebled life (live in casket)
              —Fear of separation (who will take care of me now?)
Ages 5 to 9   —Personification (bogey man)
              —Catastrophic, powerful force (death picks you out)
              —"It's not fair"—may be avoided by behavior (good or bad)
              —Not universal (I won't die)
Ages 9 to 12 —Permanent, personal, universal
              —Will die some day
              —Fascinated by the macabre (details of death, horror stories, blood and guts)
Early adolescence —Fearful yet fascinated
              —Adult understanding of death
              —Strong, intense emotions
              —Death is an enemy

—Represents the loss of a newly discovered me
—Testing the limits of life (chicken)

Ways Children React to Grief and Loss

All children/people react differently, but some of the most common reactions are:

Anger (at dead person, parents, God, self)
Feelings of abandonment (Why did you leave me?)
Guilt (my fault . . . magic wishes)
Bodily distress, e.g., upset stomach, headache (even when there are no words for our feelings, there are feelings to express)
Envy, jealousy (attention)
Regression (return to a safer time)
Increased dependency upon significant adults
Silence, withdrawal
Panic (who will take care of me now?)
Depression (lack of interest in anything)

Help for Healing the Hurt

Listen (to unspoken as well as spoken language).
Realize responses may not be obvious or immediate. (It takes time for feelings to show; just because we look "better" doesn't mean we are.)
Give permission to hurt. Destroy the myth about being strong.
Help children find constructive outlets for energy, anger, tears.
Be available. Don't turn away.
Remember that children and young people will continue to deal with their loss as they grow and mature. The loss will be addressed again and again as they gain new understandings and insights.
Bereaved children must establish a new identity. (who am I now?)

I felt lonely. My brother was gone forever. I didn't understand the conspiracy of silence, but I did understand that it wasn't something I should talk about. Thus began a silence I could sense everywhere. No one except my Mom and Dad would allow me to speak of my brother . . . I began to wonder as the years went by if I really had ever had a brother.

We left in place the pictures we had of Austin and drew comfort from seeing them. But slowly we realized that others did not feel as we did and gradually the pictures found their way into the den and the bedroom. I think that most people would have been more comfortable if we had never again spoken of Austin.

We began to pick up the pieces of our lives and I returned to the usual round of swimming, gymnastics, and after-school activities. We looked like every other family on the block . . . but inside we were different. Every day we were reminded of the emptiness that Austin's death brought to our family. No longer did we have to chart medicines or plan our activities around the whims of a malignant brain tumor. We were free to come and go as we chose. It was easier to be spontaneous, but we felt empty and hollow.

I began to worry about things. I often wondered if some other disasters could strike us. What if I got sick? Could I die, too? I did get sick with an ear infection several weeks after Big A's death. I was terribly ill and ended up at the hospital emergency room with a severe drug reaction to penicillin. My fears were coming true! The look on Mom's face confirmed that terror. Unlike Austin, I did recover, but it left me with a deep mistrust of the world and how it is supposed to work. I knew from a very early age that nothing is fair. Nothing can truly protect me, not even my Mom and Dad.

Because we were a military family, we moved frequently and I was constantly faced with starting over again in new neighborhoods, new schools, and new circles of friends. Always I was asked how many brothers and sisters did I have . . . and what pain that innocent question brought to me! Many times I decided to say I didn't have any, that I was an only child. It seemed easier that way, but I was always left with an empty feeling inside. It was as if I had negated my brother's existence. If I chose to say I had a brother but he died, then I was faced with stares, giggles, questions, and sometimes a turned back. Neither response seemed right. I would often come home filled with anger after the first day of school. I hated my Mom and Dad for making me face new beginnings over and over again, and I hated them even more for having had another child who didn't live. Didn't they know how much that hurt me? Didn't they know how lonely I felt and how fearful I was?

Of course they knew, but just as they were powerless to prevent Austin's death, they were helpless in the face of my own personal dilemma. These were feelings and thoughts that I had to address by myself. They understood my loneliness and anger and accepted my feelings and actions. They knew the struggle to find a way to live with what had happened would be my own. They gave me time and support and love and patience. They gave me silence and voice, hugs and freedom to reach an inner peace with myself.

How hard it must have been to let me struggle. How difficult it must be to know you cannot protect your children from the adult world, the hurts that are lurking around every corner. I know now of my mother's inner struggles to let me experience those corners. She let me learn to ride a bike, a snowmobile, and to ski. My dad let me disappear into the woods for weeks at a time to discover the joys of sleep-away camp. How empty my bed must have looked! They let me be a crossing guard to protect other children while placing my own safety at risk. What gifts they gave me by allowing me to grow away from them.

One of the gifts my parents gave me was the opportunity to experience whatever occurred in the world. They allowed and even encouraged me to acknowledge my feelings and to identify the causes of those feelings. Many times there was nothing to be done about those emotions except to let them flow into and out of my existence. I learned I did not have the power to change some things that happen, but I do have *the power to change the way those things affect me.*

We did not suffer in silence in my family. We talked and talked until the tears changed to laughter and painful memories faded into pleasant ones. We will never forget every moment of my brother's life, but the moments of his death now bring less hurt because we openly shared them until the sting was soothed.

Who am I now that my brother is dead? Who am I now that I have experienced the ultimate pain of losing a loved one? Who am I now that the back seat is all mine? Who am I now that I stand before you, sharing my feelings and my life?

I am Alicia Marie Sims, just as I was at the moment of my birth and just as I will be at the last breath of my life. Crisis and trauma, celebration and change do not bring about vast changes in the personality or make-up of a person. I did not grow taller or shrink because of my experiences. I am not smarter or incapacitated because of my brother's illness and death. I am who I am because of all of these things and because of the way I learned to live with them. My crises are no more dramatic than those of any other person, but they are my experiences to do with as I so choose. It is in the choosing of how to deal with the experiences we are given that we find growth of the spirit. It is not in the experience itself, but rather in the reactions to the experience that we create bitterness, anger, or compassion and the commitment to search for joy. We cannot change what happens to us, but we *can change how we deal with those things that happen.* I am not a victim of life. I may not always be pleased or joyous with the choices I have, but I am aware that I do have choices, and that knowledge is my power.

Because my parents helped me experience not only the joy of being a big sister but the jealousy, anger, helplessness, and envy of having to share my life with someone else, I have grown to know that all those feelings are acceptable. I have come to know that I can call upon my own strengths to fulfill my own dreams. I am no longer shocked that I could experience some things and I accept even those dark parts of me that I wish did not exist. Because of my brother's death, I have learned to accept the unacceptable and to use whatever may come around the corner, rather than spend the days wishing something else had drifted by.

Am I still a big sister? You bet I am! I've grown up without you, little brother. You are the pictures in the scrapbook, memories in my heart, and music in my flute. You are a part of me and I don't need the scrapbook to remember you. Maybe that's why there aren't many tears anymore. I didn't lose you, baby brother. You really are a part of me. You are the part of love that never goes away.

4

Working with Bereaved Teenagers

Louise A. Allen

A major concern of bereaved families is what to do with adolescents who are grieving. Only in recent years has our society even acknowledged that children grieve. The need for counseling and peer support for teenagers continues to be apparent. Of the peer support groups we have developed in Windsor, Ontario, the ones for teens are the most difficult to work with in terms of assisting the teens with expressing their feelings and communicating grief reactions. Teenagers give out all kinds of signals that they are experiencing difficulty adjusting to a death, and yet adults and friends are not prepared to address them. The grieving adolescent who returns to school following the death of a loved one is subject to considerable social pressure to demonstrate a resolution of grief, and to do so according to an unrealistic time table. Teens are forced into new roles: they are told to "be strong" for the surviving parent. They do not even know if they will survive themselves, let alone have enough strength to support someone else. If adequate support systems were available and teaching staff in schools were prepared for grieving students, a multitude of situational stresses could be faced or avoided.

When a parent, friend, or relative dies, a teenager feels the heavy loss of a major support system. This can overwhelm the child who will feel immobilized, with nowhere to turn. We find that teens who enter the peer support group deal with not only the negative aspects of bereavement, but begin to see that there are positive lessons from this devastating life experience. They learn they have strengths that they were not aware of having. As they discuss in group difficult individual situations, they learn coping skills and discover untapped strengths within themselves. They experience personal growth and healthy maturity. Teens learn that sometimes a couple of years are needed before healing occurs and the circle of grief is completed. This is important to acknowledge, especially because we tend to see young people in grief as strong, vibrant, and healthy individuals who would not possibly succumb to deep emotions.

Some teenagers try to postpone the pain of the process of working through grief. This can be dangerous because it can change their whole way of life and cause emotional and physical upsets. We see this every day with referrals of bereaved persons to psychiatric units. Their psychiatrists feel they are here because of grief repressed or unresolved in their younger years. Perhaps the depression, poor mental health, or suicidal thoughts would never have taken hold if someone had assisted them to deal with their grief at the time the death occurred.

Peer support groups for bereaved teenagers are proving to be excellent primary prevention programs. If approached with a sensitive understanding of what is happening to him/her emotionally, the teenager will usually acknowledge that in fact this death has created an enormous impact on his/her life.

Over the years we have asked teenagers to tell us how the support group has helped. Following are some comments:

"I know it's normal to think about my father's dead body and what happens to it."
"I've learned the importance and the pain of expressing feelings."
"I know I'm not alone."
"Now I can help someone else."
"I know some day I will be happy again."
"Talking about memories and good times helps."
"I have energy for studying again."
"I don't feel embarrassed to cry."
"There is no right or wrong way to grieve."

When we hear such words, we know that lives are becoming whole again. When a group of bereaved teens are talking and listening to one another even though the rest of the world may have stopped doing so, we know that healing is taking place.

Individual Assessment

The process for entering the support group is as follows:

1) A referral comes into the agency from a professional person, another agency, a school, place of work, or emergency ward. Anyone can refer a client as long as the client agrees. If the teenager refers him/herself on the telephone, counseling begins immediately with a bereavement specialist. A lot of listening takes place and a meeting time and place is established in that first phone call. At the same time, intake information is documented.

2) At the first one-to-one meeting the adolescent's grieving process is assessed, feelings are identified, and important concerns and problems are listed. The staff person does a lot of listening and helps the griever understand the

overwhelming tumult of emotions. In many cases hugs take place between the teen and the staff person, for often no one has hitherto recognized the need for this simple gesture.

3) The teen is then told about the adolescent peer support group. It is explained who is currently in the group, why they are there, and how it has helped particular individuals. Also, topics for group meetings and the mechanics of when and where meetings take place are discussed.

4) Meeting with the client closes with an invitation to join the next group meeting or to participate in further one-to-one meetings. Printouts with topics of meetings, a program brochure, and a brochure about grief emotions are left with the client. In parting, the staff person arranges an appropriate follow-up phone call and leaves her phone number in case the teenager wants to call.

Group Meetings

A series of 10 to 12 group meetings are held and then the series begins again. Meetings are open so that newly bereaved teens can enter at any point. If, after the series is completed, a teen wishes to start again and attend the sessions, she/ he may do so. Concurrently, the group leader (the bereavement specialist) monitors the progress of group participants on a monthly basis. The type of involvement needed by the client is noted: one-to-one support, telephone support, attendance at discussion group and social functions. Next, the phase of mourning is determined, *e.g.*, numbness, yearning, searching, anger, despair, and periods of recovery.

A coding system is used to monitor specific areas of concern such as nutrition, sleep, behavior changes, life-style adjustment, schoolwork, and isolation from friends.

Sample of Topics for Group Discussion

1. Reviewing the death experience
2. Feelings of grief
3. How the death affects you—at home, at school, with friends
4. Family meeting
5. Special needs during grief
6. Collage work/art work
7. Re-investing: new relationships, new experiences
8. Coping skills, new goals—Moving on . . .

5

Adolescents' Reactions to the Death of a Parent

Catherine E. Cragg, M.Ed and Helene A. Berman, MS, RN

Four years ago, we conducted a review of the literature on childhood bereavement. Expecting no fewer than five pages of articles addressing the subject, we were dismayed when the librarian handed us one page and told us apologetically, "I'm sorry, but this is all there is." Our initial dismay was quickly tempered by a feeling of anticipation and importance: We were about to embark on the study of some relatively untouched territory. But our overwhelming reaction was one of concern. Why had there not been more studies addressing the needs of children and adolescents whose parents had died? It is widely agreed that the death of a parent is one of the most traumatic events that can occur during childhood. Why, then, had such an important issue received so little attention? This gap seemed even more surprising in light of the extensive body of literature addressing the needs of parents when a child is terminally ill.

In this chapter we shall describe our study and share some of our findings, as well as those of other researchers. We conclude with a discussion about some of the study's implications for health professionals.

The purpose of this descriptive study was to understand more fully the experience of adolescents whose parents were diagnosed with cancer, focusing on three nodal points: the time of diagnosis of cancer, the time of the parent's death, and after the parent's deqth. Specific questions that guided this study were:

1. What types of communication patterns are used by families facing the death of a parent?
2. To what extent do each of the following variables influence the grieving process?
    A. Parents' attitudes toward death

    B. Adolescents' preparation for, and involvement in, funeral activities
    C. Changes in home and family roles
    D. Support systems
  3. What support systems are available to adolescents before, during, and after the death of a parent?

Most of the research carried out over the past 20 years has identified the negative long-term effects of parental death. Behavioral disturbances, including running away from home, poor school performance, withdrawal, and drug abuse have been reported by many researchers (Wellisch 1979; Markusen and Fulton 1971). Evidence of long-term problems was presented by Adam (1973) and Birtchnell (1970), who showed that adult psychiatric patients who had lost a parent during childhood had a higher incidence of suicidal behavior than those from intact families. Many other studies have reported a strong correlation between childhood parental loss and experience of depression and other emotional disturbances during adulthood (Dennehy 1966; Brown 1966; Adam et al. 1982).

Several problems become apparent when considering the implications of these studies. Because the populations were drawn from inpatient psychiatric hospitals, it is unclear to what the extent the findings can be applied to other groups. Also, these studies often treat those who have experienced parental loss as a homogeneous group. Whether loss follows separation, divorce, prolonged illness, or sudden death, it seems probable that family responses will vary depending on the reason.

Western culture has traditionally treated the topic of death as taboo. In an effort to "protect" young people from painful feelings and emotions, adults often avoid any discussion about death, and exclude children and adolescents from funeral activities (Grollman 1972; Wass 1986). The result of these well-intentioned, but misguided efforts may be to create more confusion and distress. Some recent studies suggest that attitudes are beginning to change and that discussions about death are becoming more acceptable (Belle-Isle 1979). With this background in mind, we will now turn to a discussion of our qualitative study.

Methodology

Semistructured interviews were conducted with 10 adolescents and their surviving parents from seven families in which a parent had died of cancer. Despite the cooperation of the local cancer clinic and palliative care unit, we had great difficulty identifying potential informants because medical records of deceased cancer patients included very little family information. All interviews took place between six months and two years after the parent's death. The adolescents were between 11 and 17 years of age when the parent died. They had no history of medical or psychological problems, and came from families that were together before the parent died. We also interviewed the surviving parent simultaneously.

We developed interview schedules to explore factors that earlier studies had indicated were important in adjusting to the loss of a parent. Appropriateness of the questions was assessed by a head nurse in the cancer clinic, a social worker, and a psychologist, all of whom had had extensive experience working with cancer patients and adolescents.

The interviews of parents and adolescents were similar. Both addressed events and reactions when the parent was diagnosed as having cancer, at death, and afterward. The adolescents were asked questions like: What were you told about your parent's illness? What kinds of changes occurred at home and school? Who helped you prepare for your parent's death? Did you participate in funeral plans? The adolescents were also asked about changes in structure, roles, and expectations within the family. They identified individuals or groups who were most supportive to them.

The surviving parents were asked similar questions about the adolescent's preparation for, and participation in, the spouse's death. They were asked about the extent to which the illness and death were discussed in the family. Parents also identified the individuals or groups they perceived as being most helpful to the adolescent. We analyzed the data independently to identify themes and commonalities. We then compared our categories and resorted the data a second time to insure some objectivity in the interpretation of the informants' answers.

Results

Demographic Data

Five boys and five girls ranging in age from 11 to 17 participated in the study. Four fathers and three mothers had died of cancer after illnesses lasting from 6 to 60 months. All the families lived in single-family dwellings in or near the city. One family had been forced to move and had lost socioeconomic status as a result of the parent's illness, but for the other six families, housing, school, and socioeconomic circumstances remained unchanged. The surviving parents in these families were employed before the death and continued to work afterward. All families were middle class; except for a black West Indian girl adopted by a white family, all were white Canadians of European descent. All the families were Protestant. The reported importance of religion ranged from not being a part of the family's life to being extremely important for all members.

Communications Among Family Members

Adolescents and parents in all the families reported that they had openly discussed the parent's illness and possible death. Major events like the diagnosis, death, and funeral were remembered and reported similarly by parents and adolescents. The adolescents said that they had been told the diagnosis and prognosis, were informed by their parents of changes in condition throughout the illness, and had participated in funeral plans and activities. All the adolescents had talked about death within their families. Seven had talked with the dying parent. For many of them, this had been a significant event in adjusting to their loss.

When the parent died, most of the families were together. Four of the adolescents were at the hospital. The others were told as soon as possible by family members. They reported feelings of shock, sadness, and relief when they realized death had come.

Communication patterns between the surviving parents and the adolescents changed after the parent died. Discussion within the families decreased. Some adolescents reported that they feared that talking about their feelings would upset their surviving parents and they protected the parent by not talking within the family. In most families, talk about the deceased parent came up incidentally. For example, if household tasks needed to be done, the family would say, "If Dad (or Mom) was here. . . ."

Changes in the Adolescents' Lives

Whereas parents and adolescents alike reported changes in household routines and responsibilities, their perceptions were often quite different. Seven of the teenagers said they were expected to assume more household responsibilities while the parent was ill, but only one parent mentioned this. After the parent's death, five of the adolescents felt that their responsibilities around the house had increased, while only one parent shared this perception. Two adolescents said that they had less freedom while their parent was ill. They were expected to stay home more and saw less of their friends.

Despite indications from the literature that behavioral and health changes often occur (Wellish 1979; Markusen and Fulton 1971), the adolescents and parents in the study reported few problems. Neither parents nor adolescents reported any increase in illness or change in schoolwork during the period of the parent's illness. Only one adolescent experienced sleeplessness before her parent's death and another girl reported having nightmares after the death. One mother stated that her son had become more demanding after his father died.

Many of the changes the families reported after the death could be seen as positive. The adolescents were able to resume the activities and developmental tasks that had been restricted during the parent's illness. Schoolwork improved for two adolescents; others reported more freedom. Four parents said their children had become involved in more activities outside the house.

Supports for the Adolescents

The adolescents and parents were asked to identify who had been supportive to the adolescents during and after the illness. Adolescents tended to report that people the family had known previously were most helpful. Support often took the form of practical help such as sending in meals and mowing the lawn. Parents and adolescents within the same family often differed considerably in their identification of supports. Parents attributed more help to doctors and school officials than did the adolescents. The parents were less aware of support from siblings, whereas the adolescents perceived their siblings as sharing similar emotions and thus as being an important source of support.

The adolescents talked with siblings and friends about their feelings throughout the process, but especially after the death, when they were reluctant to talk to the parents. Friends were identified as supportive, but some of the adolescents reported that it was difficult to turn to peers who had not experienced the loss of a parent. In two families, meeting other adolescents who had lost a parent was helpful.

The adolescents reported little or no contact with the health care professionals who cared for their parents. They perceived that the professionals were important sources of support for their parents, but seldom for themselves. Parents, on the other hand, believed that the health care professionals who had helped them were also helpful to their children. In families where religion was important, the adolescents identified clergy and church contacts as supportive.

Discussion

We were surprised and pleased to find that our findings contrasted with previous indications that families avoid talking about death with children and adolescents (Grollman 1972; Wass 1986). The families in this study discussed the subject openly while the parent was ill and included their teenagers in funeral plans and rituals. Influences of different communication patterns on the reactions of adolescents could not be assessed because of the similarities of experiences reported by the families.

Based on what is known about grief and mourning (Furman 1985; Lindemann 1944), the young people who participated in this study appeared to be dealing effectively with their loss. The communication patterns established before the parent died probably helped the adolescents cope effectively with a painful experience. Although grief was evident, all the adolescents we interviewed talked freely about their parent, remembering the good and bad times. They had readjusted to their environment, formed new relationships, and developed new interests. Most of the surviving parents reported their adolescents were more mature.

Some adolescents felt isolated by the experience. The surviving parents were preoccupied with the illness or with grieving, and the adolescents wanted to protect them. The great variation in parents' and adolescents' reports of who was supportive may reflect the parents' inability to be sensitive to the adolescents' needs when they themselves were emotionally drained. There was some reversal of roles as the children assumed more responsibility and protected their parents. Peers could not understand something they themselves had not experienced. Health professionals and teachers were seen as remote. Although adolescents turned to relatives and friends, they reported feeling "different" and needing other outlets.

Limitations of the Study

Major limitations of the study include the small number of families involved, and the geographic, religious, ethnic, and socioeconomic homogeneity of the informants. They came from one geographic area and were not randomly selected. There was self-selection of the informants because only those who volunteered were interviewed. Probably only those who felt comfortable talking about the experience responded to our requests. Since all the parents died of cancer after illnesses of months or years, findings cannot be generalized to other causes of death and lengths of illness. Because all interviews were conducted less than two years after the parent's death, long-term outcomes for these adolescents and their families are unknown.

Implications

Despite the aforementioned limitations, the results of this study indicate a number of implications for those involved with families with a terminally ill parent and adolescent children.

Awareness. Identify the family composition and communication patterns in order to help adolescents participate in the dying process. Assess the ability and readiness of the family to discuss illness and death. Encourage an atmosphere of open communication to assist the adolescent's adjustment. Provide adolescents with accurate and honest information and be aware that they may need opportunities to express feelings of sadness, anger, and guilt outside the family.

Because adolescents turn first to those they know, it is important to help the family identify and mobilize the supports that already exist for them. Identify changes in home and family roles and responsibilities, and the feelings created by such changes. Many adolescents may welcome the opportunity to assume increased responsibility in household activities. However, they should be recognized for their efforts by parents and those involved with the family. Assess whether extra responsibilities are limiting adolescents' opportunities for independence and peer-group activities and discuss this with parents and adolescents.

Realize that surviving parents may not be perceiving the responses and needs of their children accurately. Seek out the adolescents and speak with them individually if necessary.

Records. The health records of cancer patients should include the number and ages of the children at home and should incorporate information on what family members know about the illness, and how they are reacting. Communication among helping professionals, both written and oral, should reflect the needs of all members of the family. Plans should take the entire family into account and professional contacts with all members should be recorded.

Follow-up. The changes we found in family communication patterns after a parent's death indicate that support for the family must not end when the parent dies. Arrange follow-up and make appropriate referrals to give adolescents a chance to resolve the feelings they are unable to express within the family. Take steps to foster resumption of effective communication patterns if these have been interrupted by the crisis of death.

Adolescents might turn to peers for support, but usually feel their friends do not understand. Forming peer support groups for adolescents may help them cope with the problem of having a terminally ill parent, before and after the death.

Further Research. The effect of parental death on adolescents needs to be further researched. Information should be collected from larger numbers of subjects from a variety of geographic locations, and from different socioeconomic, ethnic, and religious backgrounds. Studies should be undertaken to determine the reactions of adolescents who lose a parent to causes other than cancer and on the effect of sudden death rather than prolonged illness. Further research on peer support groups should also be undertaken to determine their effectiveness.

References

Adam, K. 1973. Childhood parental loss, suicidal ideation, and suicidal behaviour. In E.J. Anthony and C. Loupernik, eds. *The Child in his family: The impact of disease and death.* New York: John Wiley & Sons, pp. 275-98.

Adam, K., J. Harper and D. Steiner. 1982. Early parental loss and suicidal ideation. *Canadian Journal of Psychiatry* 27(4):275-81.

Belle-Isle, J.A. 1979. The child who loses a family member. In D.P. Hymovich and M. Underwood, eds. *Family health care* Vol. 2 (2nd ed.) New York: McGraw Hill, pp. 263-79.

Birtchnell, J. 1970. Relationship between attempted suicide, depression, and parent death. *British Journal of Psychiatry* 116:307-13.

Brown, F. 1966. Depression and childhood bereavement. *British Journal of Psychiatry* 112:1035-41.

Dennehy, C.M. 1966. Childhood bereavement. *British Journal of Psychiatry* 112:1049-69.

Furman, E. 1985. Children's patterns in mourning the death of a loved one. *Issues Comparative Pediatric Nursing* 8:205-17.

Grollman, E.A. 1972. *Talking about death: A dialogue between parent and child.* Boston: Beacon Press, pp. 3-31.

Lindemann, E. 1944. Symptomatology and management of acute grief. *American Journal of Psychiatry* 101(Sept.):141-48.

Markusen, E. and R. Fulton. 1971. Childhood bereavement and behaviour disorders; A critical review. *Omega* 2:107-17.

Wass, J. 1986. Teaching the facts of death: A living issue. In G.H. Paterson, ed. *Children and death.* London, Ontario: King's College, pp. 7-19.

Wellisch, D.K. 1979. Adolescent acting out when a parent has cancer. *International Journal of Family Therapy* 1:230-41.

6

When an Alcoholic Parent Dies

Lynne Martins, BA

The impending or actual death of a parent is a traumatic event for any child. The loss of a parent poses a direct threat to the child's emotional and physical security. The uncertainty of the future is now the playground for exacerbated anxieties and separation issues. However, in an alcoholic home, chaos and uncertainty are everyday occurrences. Unpredictability, unreliability, and inconsistency are the fabric by which a child learns to pattern his/her own survival techniques and coping mechanisms for the daily crises of life. The loss issues peculiar to an alcoholic home are legion. Coupled with the actual loss of a parent by death, grief issues rage out of control as these children are left not only to cope with the actual death, but with the years of loss they have known due to the behavior and environment created by a parents' addiction to alcohol.

It is essential for the surviving parent, counselor, teacher, or other helping professionals to be aware of the ramifications these intense loss issues have on a bereaved child. Often, these clients are seen as difficult, resistant individuals who need long-term therapy. Progress is slow and often feels incomplete. Because the issues are complex and sometimes misunderstood by the helping professional, therapy is sometimes a frustrating experience for both the therapist and the client.

The intent of this chapter is to inform and enlighten the helping professional regarding the loss issues that are concurrent with the grief process of a child of an alcoholic parent (COA). This chapter will cover the following four major areas: (a) understanding the alcoholic home: rules and roles; (b) losses inherent in an alcoholic home; (c) complications within the grief process; and (d) treatment methods and strategies.

Understanding the Alcoholic Home

The Rules

It is essential to understand how the dynamics and elements of an alcoholic home contribute to the complication of the grief process for a COA. The structure of the home is generally set up in a kind of order, or shall I say, disorder. The two constituents that contribute to the disorder are the rules and the roles.

In a healthy, loving home, rules are set down or negotiated with the best interest of each person in mind. In an alcoholic home, three rules become the fabric by which the means for survival are established and the system of denial is perpetuated. As outlined by Dr. Claudia Black, author of *It'll Never Happen to Me* (1982), these rules are:

Don't talk: This rule is first and foremost. Children are not allowed to discuss what they perceive or experience within the home. Equally important, children are not allowed to discuss "family problems" with anyone outside of the family system. The family "secret" is defended at all costs.

Don't trust: This rule follows closely on the heels of the first rule. Children who learn not to talk about what is actually occurring in the home learn to question their own ability to perceive things correctly. They inherently doubt themselves and their automatic response to others is mistrust.

Don't feel: This rule is adopted as an ultimate means of survival. To feel would subject a child to a sense of powerlessness, helplessness, and incredible pain on a regular basis. To combat the daily chaos, feeling is not a viable option. For a child, it becomes too great a risk to feel. Feelings are something expressed for another, but not for oneself.

The Roles

With the rules rigidly intact, family members must find coping mechanisms to be able to adhere to the rules. Each person chooses a definite role that serves a dual purpose: the role becomes a coping mechanism for the individual and also serves to maintain the delicate balance necessary for the family system to exist. The participants in these roles are known as:

The Alcoholic: The person abusing alcohol.

The Co-Alcoholic: usually the spouse, also referred to as the "enabler" or "rescuer." This person is primarily preoccupied with the behavior of the alcoholic. As the co-alcoholic is part of a conspiracy of denial that enables the alcoholism to continue, he/she hides the evidence of the alcoholism or denies the behavior of the alcoholic.

The Family Hero Child: the child who takes on the responsibility of the family. Usually somewhat of a "junior parent," this child takes on an inordinate amount of responsibility for the physical and emotional well-being of the other members of the family.

The Scapegoat Child: the child who acts out the family pain by being a "troublemaker." Is seen as a misfit.

The Placater Child: the flip-side of the Scapegoat. This child seeks to be the family comforter. Wants to make everyone "feel" better; absorbs the family pain.

The Lost Child: the "angel" child. This is the child whose name is easily forgotten; always in the background, never causes trouble. This child feels nothing.

The Mascot/Clown Child: this child is generally tense, anxious, overactive, deflecting the pain of the family by constantly keeping everyone entertained and laughing.

The roles are interchangeable. Once a role has been relinquished, it is common for another family member to assume the abandoned role to ensure the maintenance of the family structure. It is also common for family members to vacillate between more than one role. The death of a parent does little to interfere with this intense loyalty and protection of the "family secret" regardless of the cost to an individual. In many instances, the death of a parent actually reinforces the incessant drive to keep the system going.

Losses Inherent in an Alcoholic Home

The Loss of Self

When survival hinges on the mastery of a certain role, there is little room for the "real" self to emerge. When affirmation of personhood is absent, children often suffer a sense of meaninglessness or lostness in life. It is difficult for them to believe that they impact another's life in a positive way—or in any way at all.

The Loss of Childhood

For a COA, childhood is not a time of freedom, exploration, and affirmation. Spontaneity is often absent. Childhood is preoccupied with caring for other children and/or their parents. This loss demonstrates itself in a child's intense seriousness about, and inability to enjoy, life.

The Loss of Developmental Stages

Developmental stages are often thwarted or denied due to the fact that a child's existence is an extension of the alcoholic parent or the co-alcoholic parent's needs or addictions. For example, the chart below reflects the differences between a normal home and an alcoholic home during the stage of development known as autonomy.

NORMAL ATMOSPHERE	ALCOHOLIC ATMOSPHERE
1. New relationships with both both males & females are encouraged.	*Isolation:* any person outside of the family structure is seen as a "threat" to the structure. An objective outsider is likely to see the denial and problems within the family. *Mistrust of others:* Children are taught that they cannot trust anyone. Since they have learned not to trust the alcoholic person, it seems logical to mistrust other people.
2. Exploration and integration of new stimuli or situations are encouraged.	New situations are met with much anxiety and apprehension. The lack of control associated with new situations give rise to enormous fear.
3. Self-perceptions are encouraged and affirmed.	Self perceptions are not validated but dismissed; the truth is denied, criticized or minimized: "How dare you say that! Dad/Mom isn't drunk, he/she's just a little sick with the flu."
4. Home is a "safe" environment in which to test perceptions and new found freedoms.	There is no safe place in which a child can express or test perceptions. Suppression or a "numbing out" of emotions is learned at an early age.

Autonomy is one of the basic components for the development of a healthy ego. Autonomy is one example of the many stages of development that may be sacrificed within the confines of an alcoholic environment.

Loss of Parents (Prior to Actual Death)

The many disappointments, broken promises, and shattered dreams inherent in an alcoholic home initiate the COA into the grieving process at an early age. Perhaps the most crazy-making aspect of all is the loss of both parents without an actual death occurring. The alcoholic parent is emotionally and often physically unavailable for the child. The co-alcoholic's concern with the alcoholic's behavior and his/her own responses to the addictive partner leave another type of absence with which the child must cope.

Early on, a child begins to grieve for "what is." Due to a limited understanding of what is normal, coupled with isolation, a child feels very sad for the way the family is, but she does not have the intellectual maturity to realize that the situation is grossly abnormal. As a child grows older, a new layer of grief comes with the exposure to peers and other family models. This exposure both validates the awful truth that the COA's family is "different" and reinforces the sense of powerlessness the child feels at not being able to change their own situation. She begins to grieve for what "cannot be." The loss of an "idealized" parent (and family) is further complicated as she assumes responsibility for the alcoholism in the family, concluding that she has brought this terrible disaster upon herself.

Complications within the Grief Process

There are many theories about the stages or phases of grief work. While the author understands that the model presented by Kubler-Ross is primarily for adult grief processes, this familiar model has been integrated with Claudia Jewett's work with children's grief processes. The result is the model below, which is sufficient to compare the grief processes of children from a stable environment and those who come from an alcoholic home.

PHASE I: DENIAL AND SHOCK

NORMAL RESPONSE

COA RESPONSE

Flatness; robotlike, mechanical behavior broken by outbursts of panic.

Prolonged flatness, indifference to death. Absence of tears or expression of emotions.

Casual response of indifference. Hyperactivity as a form of denial.

Little alarm for self expressed—has developed a high tolerance for turmoil and chaos. Developed a protective layer to take care of self.

Extended denial of actual death. Has difficulty distinguishing between actual death and instances related to alcoholic episodes (chronic absenteeism/passing out).

Extended period of denial may be exhibited in the drive of over-achievement, increased behavioral problems, or increased isolation depending upon the role of the child within the family.

Denial is a double-pronged response for a COA: 1) denial of the disease and 2) denial of the actual death.

PHASE TWO: SADNESS/ANGER/SHAME

NORMAL RESPONSE

COA RESPONSE

Duration is 6–12 weeks, but completion of adjustment is estimated at around 2 years.

It is difficult to estimate the "normal" duration of these emotions since the issues are so closely related to dysfunction of an alcoholic home.

Duration of this grief phase has a direct correlation with resolution of subsequent losses the child experienced prior to the actual death of the parent.

1. *Sadness:* child is withdrawn, despondent, tearful.

Sadness: no response at all or exaggerated response that does not match the response of peers.

2. *Anger:* child has difficulty in expressing anger. Anger is perceived as additional threat of withdrawal of love. Child imagines the reaction to his anger to be one of desertion, retribution or injury.
Feelings may be so intense that the child may feel like he is going "crazy."
Need to retaliate: child feels that the person they most trusted betrayed him by dying.

Anger: same as a normal response, but underlying fear that the expression of anger may be a statement of disloyalty or betrayal of the deceased parent. Anger may be displaced onto self as a type of punishment and be exhibited in the forms of passive-aggressive behavior; chronic sadness/depression; acting out or some type of substance abuse (compulsive eating, alcohol, drugs).

3. *Shame:* death is perceived as reflection of self. Children tend to believe that death is a form of abandonment: "Dad died because I was such a bad child."

Shame: same for COA. In addition, a COA would feel shame for self. Shame is associatied with actual existence. Child is unable to distinguish self from parental behavior and often feels shame for being alive.

PHASE THREE: BARGAINING/GUILT

NORMAL RESPONSE

Bargaining: Children bargain with statements such as "I'll be the best little boy/girl in the world" or "You'll see. If I wait long enough, they'll come back."

Guilt: Children often assume responsibility for the loss, especially in magical thinking stage of development (4–7 yrs.)

A parents' death is a terrible blow to self image: "I am so bad, my own parents didn't want me."

COA RESPONSE

Bargaining: Same as normal response except that the sense of helplessness, powerlessness, and despair are reinforced. Having grown up bargaining for a parent's sobriety, a deep sense of hopelessness develops.

Guilt: A child assumes responsibility for the alcoholism, chaos, and ultimately for the death. Guilt is deeply ingrained and exacerbated especially if the death is alcohol related.

Guilt takes another form as feelings of ambivalence toward the death surface. A sense of relief may be felt by the child, but confusion, guilt, and depression soon replace the feelings of relief. Prolonged guilt manifests itself in an inability to enjoy life and resume activities that once brought pleasure.

PHASE FOUR: DESPAIR/DEPRESSION/DISORGANIZATION

NORMAL RESPONSE

Despair: A hopeless, bleak state: "The worst thing has happened and I am helpless to change it." Normal duration can range from a few days to a few weeks. Normal interests are diminished. Extreme fatigue; slow moving, pessimistic, lack of motivation. Child will be very dependent; needs to feel protected.

COA RESPONSE

Despair: same as normal response but complicated with the following messages: "The worst possible thing has happened, I should have been able to stop it. I am helpless to change it, and furthermore, I caused it."

The normal duration of this stage is very difficult to determine.

Withdrawal leads to further isolation and depression.

Lack of dependency is expressed due to the learned mistrust of others.

Depression: is closely connected to despair. A push-pull feeling of the need to relinquish what has been lost and a need to hold on.

Children fear that they will "forget" about the deceased parent.

Depression: is displayed in at least two forms: 1) depression for "what could never be" and 2) depression for "what will never be."

Unresolved guilt (authentic or inauthentic) will have a direct correlation with the depression. Depression results from feelings of ambivalence toward the death of the parent coupled with guilt over having feelings or thoughts of relief.

Regression of behavior to an earlier stage of development that was mastered or presumed "safe."

Absence of depression: grief becomes one more obstacle to master. Child may display super-human ability to cope with loss and, in turn, the child mourns vicariously. May feel empathy for another family member, but not for self.

Needs more sleep but suffers from increased sleep disturbances.

Inability to rest well or relax.

Regression is chastised: "You're the man/woman of the family now, you've got to be strong." Child expected to assume additional responsibility to care for other members of the family.

Disorganization: this stage can last for more than 1 year.

Disorganization: Disorganization: the symptoms are the same as a normal response. However, the duration of the disorganization is longer and of chronic proportions. The child may already be having difficulty in school: the death accentuates any learning or behavioral problems the child is experiencing.

There is a lack of motivation demonstrated in aimlessness, lack of concentration, and inability to follow directions. Disorganization manifests itself as children become forgetful of how to accomplish tasks that were once easily mastered.

Withdrawn in general, children exhibit an increased passivity.

Daydreaming is a normal response. Unfortunately, daydreaming children are often labeled as "lazy."

The development of a fantasy life/reading books is a means of escape for adolescents.

Reduced ability to cope due to isolation, limited resources upon which to draw from, and possible drug or alcohol abuse as means of escape.

PHASE FIVE: SEARCHING/INTEGRATION/ADJUSTMENT

Searching is a vital step in the adjustment to the death of a parent. Searching is the beginning to make sense of the loss so as to integrate and adjust to the loss. Unfortunately this stage is often missed or met with intolerance. This is one of the most difficult stages for adults to watch a child process.

NORMAL RESPONSES

Searching: preoccupation with deceased; waiting for "clue" as to where to find the deceased parent. Searching subsides but does not cease until every attempt at reunion is unsuccessful.

Integration of Loss: The worst possible thing happened and I survived it. Average integration 18 months.

COA RESPONSES

Searching: same as normal response. The preoccupation of the deceased may reach pathological proportions if the child begins to express intentions of reunion with the deceased parent by death (suicide).

Integration of Loss: depends upon the integration and attention given to the subsequent losses the COA has experienced. Without dealing with the subsequent losses, the COA has little hope of integration of the death of the parent. Grief goes underground indefinitely.

Restored self-esteem.

Restored ability to enjoy life.

Can integrate caring, healthy relationships.

Adjustment: the ability to "move on" with life. Child is able to adapt to the death and continues to adapt during difficult instances such as birthdays, holidays, and anniversary dates.

Adjustment: very difficult but adjustment is possible. Generally, it will take more time and, once agian, is dependent upon how well the child has adjusted to the subsequent losses prior to the actual death of the parent; and the acceptance of the parent's disease of alcoholism.

Birthday, holiday, and anniversary dates are met with an exaggerated response or no response at all due to the fact that the losses are not adequately resolved and each reminder triggers subsequent losses.

Pathological Symptoms

It is my opinion that COA's are prime candidates for pathological grief. Due to the inordinate amount of losses that are "stacked" and "buried" throughout childhood, COA's are generally ill-equipped for coping with traumatic losses such as death.

Due to the complexities of the subject of pathological grief, I will attempt to briefly summarize a few of the more classic symptoms.

1. Imitation of the symptoms and behavior of the deceased. This becomes pathological when the traits displace the child's own identification or is prolonged. This is especially alarming as COA's imitate the deceased parent's behavior by becoming alcoholic themselves.
2. Delayed or postponed reaction to death. Due to the denial and chaos already present in an alcoholic home, it is not uncommon for the reaction to death to be delayed indefinitely.
3. Distortions of normal grief reactions. May be a fixation on or a distortion of a certain stage of the grief process.

4. Hostility (either open or hidden)
5. Self-punitive behavior. For a COA, this can result from the guilt harbored during childhood.
6. Agitated depression that results from distorted grief: "It should have been me that died."

For a more complete understanding of pathological grief, please refer to Erich Lindemann's article, "Symptomatology and Management of Acute Grief."

Treatment Strategies

The clarity with which a helping professional offers treatment to a child is most important. There is a very high percentage of COA's in the helping professions. Coming to terms with their own denial and the losses suffered as a COA is essential to being an effective therapist. Denial that is unresolved will only undermine the therapeutic process and create further damage for the child in therapy.

Loss History Inventory

One of the most effective means of determining subsequent losses is accomplished by taking a loss history inventory. Children will respond to direct or indirect questions. For example, "You must have been very frightened when your mother told you your father died." (This helps the child identify a feeling associated with the event. "Have there been other times when you felt very frightened?" "Can you tell me about them?"

Art Therapy

The use of art forms as a strategy for therapy is very effective for COA's who find it very difficult to verbalize what they are feeling.

Play Therapy

Play therapy is another vehicle by which a therapist can facilitate a safe and trustworthy environment in which a child will express emotions. During play therapy, a therapist can observe the relational patterns of the child to other family members, self, and others.

Group Therapy

The older child may respond more favorably to a group therapy situation. Often, a child feels it a relief to know that he/she is not alone and his/her situation as a COA is not unique. Groups can provide much of the validation that is needed for the grieving process to begin.

Family Therapy

Family therapy is highly unlikely unless the co-alcoholic is seeking treatment. Often, the ''scapegoat' child is brought in as the presenting problem. While family therapy is not impossible, it is very difficult. Once the immediate crisis of bereavement has been addressed, it is wise to refer the family to a skilled chemical dependency therapist if you are unfamiliar with the issues present in an alcoholic home.

(Note: Some of the most pragmatic suggestions for helping children are found in Claudia Jewett's book, *Helping Children Cope with Separation and Loss*. I highly recommend this book.)

Conclusion

Unfortunately, the majority of COA's will continue to face the multifaceted problems of grieving in silence and isolation. Helping professionals must take the initiative to educate and incorporate strategies into grief therapy that address the larger surplus of losses innate in an alcoholic home. Acceptance of the parents' disease will be the key to moving ahead for a COA. Differentiating between self and parents will help to establish the necessary groundwork needed to deal with unresolved losses coupled with the grief process.

With the experience of a skilled therapist, COA 's can be given the validation and tools necessary to unravel the many complexities of the subsequent losses and actual death of an alcoholic parent.

References

Alcohol and the family. 1988. *Newsweek*, 111, p. 62.
Alcoholics: No place like home. 1987. *Psychology Today*, 21, p. 22.
Barnes, D. 1987. Previous losses: Forgotten but not resolved. Workshop presented at Bereavement Conference at King's College, London, Ontario, Canada.
Berkus, R. 1985. *To heal again.* Encino, CA: Red Rose.
Bernstein, R. 1986. Life without father. *Parent's Magazine*, 61, p. 110.
Black, C. and L. Dwinell. 1985. Alcohol in the family. Seminar, February 1985, Pasadena, California.
Black, C. 1982. *It will never happen to me.* Denver, CO: Mac.
Black, C. 1981. *My Dad loves me: My Dad has a disease: A workbook for children of alcoholics.*
Blankfield, A. 1982-83. Grief and alcohol. *American Journal of Drug and Alcohol Abuse* 9(4): 435-46.
Burns, D. 1980. *Feeling good: The new mood therapy.* New York: Signet.
Cantor, P. 1987. Give the bereft child a chance to grieve. *Los Angeles Times*, Los Angeles, California.
Cohn, J. 1987. The grieving student. *Instructor's Magazine* 96:76.
Colgrove, Bloomfield and McWilliams. 1976. *How to survive the loss of a love.* New York: Bantam Books.

Furman, E. 1974. *A child's parent dies.* New Haven, CN: Yale University Press.

Grollman, E. 1967. *Explaining death to children.* Boston: Beacon Press.

———1981. *What helped me when my loved one died.* Boston: Beacon Press.

Gross, B. and G. Kearney. 1987. Grief work model. Transcript from weekly lecture at St. John's Hospital, Ft. Logan Dependency Center.

Hart, A. 1987. *Counseling the depressed.* Waco, TX: Word Inc.

Hastings, J. and M. Typpo. 1984. *An elephant in the living room: The children's book and leader's guide.*

Hawkes, W. 1986. *Alcohol and the family: The breaking point.* Color Videocassette, 29 minutes with teacher's guide. AIMS Media: New York State Nurses' Association Library.

Jackson, E. 1977. *The many faces of grief.* Nashville, TN: Abingdon Press.

Jewett, C. 1982. *Helping children cope with separation and loss.* Boston: Harvard Common Press.

Kubler-Ross, E. 1970. *On death and dying.* New York: Macmillan.

———1983. *On children and death.* New York: Macmillan.

———1974. *Questions and answers on death and dying.* New York: Macmillan.

Lindemann, E. 1944. Symptomology and management of acute grief. *American Journal of Psychiatry* 101:166–81.

Manning, D. 1984. *Don't take my grief away.* New York: Harper and Row.

Marks, J. 1986. The child of alcoholics. *Parent's Magazine,* 61, p. 104.

Middleton-Moz, J. and L. Dwinell. 1986. *After the tears: Reclaiming the personal losses of childhood.* Deerfield Beach, FL: Health Communications.

Mumford, A. 1983. *Love my hurt away.* Denver, CO: Accent Expressions.

Pursche, J. 1987. Alcohol and a son's Oedipus Complex. *Los Angeles Times,* Los Angeles, California.

Royner, S. 1987. Orphans find aftereffects inexorable and painful. The *Sunday Oregonian* newspaper, Oregon.

Seixas and Youcha. *Children of alcoholism: A survivor's manual.* New York: Crown Publishers.

———1987. The longest hangover. *Philadelphia Magazine* 96.

Simos, B. 1979. *A time to grieve.* New York: Family Service Association.

Stickney, D. 1982. *Waterbugs and dragonflies.* New York: Pilgrim Press.

Wolfe, A. 1972. *Helping your child understand death.* New York: Child Study.

Worden, W. 1982. *Grief counseling and grief therapy: A handbook for the mental health practitioner.* New York: Springer Publishing Co.

7

The Impact on Adolescents When A Sibling is Dying

Eleanor J. Deveau, RN, BScN

Until recently, the needs of siblings of all ages have been overlooked in discussions of the care of children who are seriously ill and dying. Barbara Sourkes (1981) noted that siblings have the most problems and the greatest needs of all family members. When children are ill, healthy siblings are affected by all that transpires and they are profoundly affected when their brother or sister dies. Their experience will be carried with them for the remainder of their lives (Adams and Deveau 1987). Coleman and Coleman (1984) suggest that the death of a child has long been perceived as one of the most painful of family experiences. If we examine the literature, the focus is on the disease, the sick child, the parents, and the family at large. There is very limited information on adolescent siblings who are experiencing the death of a brother or sister and few guidelines concerning their role in palliative care (Adams and Deveau 1987).

In this chapter I discuss the impact on adolescent siblings when their brother or sister is dying, either at home or in the hospital. My focus is on childhood cancer, where my clinical background is strongest, although much of this information can be paralleled with other chronic illnesses resulting in death. I start by looking at sibling relationships in general, the transitions in adolescence, and adolescents' perspectives of and their reactions to dying and death. Within this context, I consider the influence of adult expectations and the difficulties that they create for adolescents. Next, I outline factors that influence adolescent vulnerability during terminal care and then turn my focus to the feelings, needs, and coping responses of these teens when their brother or sister is dying of cancer. Finally, I address factors that influence adolescents' positive or negative adjustment after a sibling's death and conclude with guidelines for intervention.

Sibling Relationships

Daily living provides a forum where siblings interact through a wide range of behaviors. Their attachments are distinct from their relationships with adults. They share secrets, they play, scheme, dream, provoke, argue, and protect each other (Bank and Kahn 1982; Adams and Deveau 1987). Sibling relationships form a subsystem that promotes socialization, companionship, role modeling, mutual support, and rivalry (Minuchin 1974; Siemon 1984; Drotar 1978; Furman and Burhmester 1985). Bank and Kahn (1982) suggest that sibling relationships are influenced by their parents, each other, biological and social change, and culture. In addition to these, I would add the impact of chronic illness and potential death.

When we consider the demands forced on families during terminal care, we can appreciate the difficulties that adolescents encounter in their roles and relationships as siblings of a dying child. These young people are placed in a quandary: How do they remain a sibling and still conform to parental expectations? Adolescent siblings must often contend with being caught in the middle: they feel empathy for both the dying child and the parent. They understand what the dying child is going through but they also recognize their parents stress and the need for the establishment of boundaries and control.

Relationship of Adolescents to their Dying Siblings

When the dying child is younger, the adolescent tends to assume a mothering role, complete with protection and overindulgence. There is little, if any, rivalry and the teen willingly defends the dying child (Penn 1983; Adams and Deveau 1987).

If the dying child is close in age or a twin, the teen may experience considerable difficulty because of close identification (Breslau 1982; Adams and Deveau 1987). These children may become preoccupied with the potential death of their sibling and the possibility of their own death. There may be jealousy and resentment as well as sadness for the loss of a partner. The greater the closeness in age of siblings, the greater the possibility for the development of serious problems during palliative care and bereavement (Bank and Kahn 1982; Osterweiss 1986).

Adolescents whose older brother or sister is dying may mourn the loss of their protector, confidant, role model, and idol.

Adolescence

Adolescents are neither children nor adults but young people who are going through a phase of life filled with rapid physical growth, sexual maturation, and specific cognitive and emotional needs (Corr and McNeil 1986). The literature has characteristically portrayed adolescence as a time of disruption, turmoil, and rebellion (Gordon 1986). Adolescence is also a time of transitions, and teens often vacillate as they struggle with their parents' and society's expectations of them. Through all this, they strive for independence and the freedom to make their own choices and decisions.

Although commonly viewed as a single phase of life, adolescence consists of three distinct phases.

Early Adolescence.   The young adolescent is capable of logical thought, tends to be dependent on parents, and is easily influenced. Role modeling is accepted; parents are still friends and sometimes even companions. These teens are more compliant to demands and more willing to work within the boundaries of parental structure. They may do some experimenting but this is influenced by culture and peers. Anxieties tend to focus on physical and sexual changes and peer relationships (Lewis 1982).

Middle Adolescence.   This phase, which coincides with age 16, is usually the peak of turmoil and rebellion. These teens are prone to emotional fluctuations and extreme reactions. They often exhibit a fight-or-flight response: girls typically shout and slam doors, while boys may isolate themselves in their rooms (Adams and Deveau 1987). Middle adolescents become judgmental, try to bargain with adults, and feel that they "know it all." Parents become their "worst enemies," peers become a priority, and they often experiment or break rules as they try to establish their own beliefs and values. As they seek their independence, they struggle with dependency needs, sexuality issues, and their own self-images (Fleming and Adolph 1986).

Late Adolescence.   Older adolescents' rationality and increasing maturity allow them to function with less denial and overt emotion than their younger counterparts. They complete their physical and sexual maturation, clarify their ethics and values, and continue to acquire adult social skills. They begin to move into new social spheres and try to find peers and perhaps a mate with the same values. As they continue to establish their own independence, they may separate from their family of origin and begin to make long-term commitments, including career decisions (Lewis 1982; Gordon 1986).

The Adolescent's Perspective on Death

Adolescents have distinct concerns and capabilities in relation to dying and death that have a separate focus from those of younger children. The early adolescent becomes aware of the personal and family implications of death, whereas the older adolescent attempts to impart meaning to death as well as to life (Gordon 1986). There is considerable transition in thought and understanding during these years.

Factors Influencing Adolescents' Reactions to Dying and Death

The following factors may influence adolescents' reactions when they have a personal experience with dying and death:

1. Avoidance of Death in Childhood.   Teens develop ways of handling life's events that are continuously being modified by their personal experiences. As children, however, many of them were screened or sheltered from any real involvement in dying and death. Such topics were usually not openly and systematically discussed (Gordon 1986). As a result, many teens have no previous history and therefore lack the preparation to cope with death (Spinetta 1981).

2. Death = Distance, Violence and Destruction.   From a societal perspective, we are still very uncomfortable with illness, dying, and death. Death is held at a distance. It is viewed as impersonal and often is depicted by the media and contemporary music as violent and destructive (Attig 1986; Gordon 1986).

3. Adolescence = Turmoil and Disruption.   Society is uncomfortable with adolescence, defining it as a time of turmoil and disruption, a time that adults often wish would pass quickly so that young people could get on with their lives (Gordon 1986).

4. Natural Communication and Relationship Dichotomy.   Sometimes the natural pattern of interaction that separates adolescents from parents and other adults may hinder open and honest communication and discussion concerning dying and death (Adams and Deveau 1986, 1987).

5. Shyness, Uncertainty, and Lack of Confidence.   These characteristics may inhibit adolescents from asking questions. They may also be misread: because they remain quiet, adults may assume that they are uninterested or do not have any questions or concerns.

6. Culture, Religion, and Ethnic Differences.   The granting of adult privileges and responsibilities varies among cultures, religions, and ethnic groups. With many, religious status is conferred during early adolescence. As a result, these young people are suddenly expected to be adult participants in religious customs and rituals concerning death.

Gordon (1986) notes that for teens, dying and death shatter any lingering "fantasies of immortality" and forces them to face the possibility of their own death. When they encounter the death of someone close, their "ideals of fairness, justice and goodness" are violated. They may also question or challenge God's existence. As one teen said:

> I don't know how I should feel . . . there's nothing we can do about all this. It's so sad . . . so permanent! Why did God make this happen to him?

7. Peer Relationships. Adolescents often turn to each other for support. Peers, however, may not be very supportive in sorting out difficult feelings because they may not have had a similar personal experience with dying and death and they may be too anxious to talk about what is happening (Gordon 1986). Mary said:

> It was hard for my friends to understand what I was going through . . . we didn't talk much about my sister's dying but I was still one of the gang and went out with them when I could.

Jeff would get together with Bill and Jamie:

> We'd go to the arcades . . . have some fun. They'd ask me if I was hanging in and how Joey was doing but we didn't really talk about things. How can they know what I'm feeling? Besides, they don't know what to say . . . they haven't been where I am.

Peer support may actually be used more as a means for "time out" or respite rather than talking about what is happening and dealing with feelings.

All of these factors have a direct bearing on the difficulties adolescents experience in coping with the death of someone close. In addition, adult expectations can create further stress.

Adult Expectations of Adolescents

Several assumptions underlie common adult expectations of adolescents. These young people are expected to be more mature than children; therefore they are expected to think rationally and understand what is happening. According to this line of thinking, adolescents should be able to handle any crisis and cope with whatever transpires. Because adolescents are capable of independent thought and action, then it may be assumed that they are less dependent on adults for assistance and guidance. And because issues related to death are seen as very personal, adolescents' privacy is upheld and they are often left on their own to manage difficult thoughts and feelings (Adams and Deveau 1987). In addition, if parents and adults impose expectations and responsibilities that are beyond adolescents' true capabilities, these teens may experience considerable difficulty coming to terms with their situation.

Difficulties Adolescents Encounter with Adult Expectations

The following expectations and responsibilities may create further difficulties for adolescent siblings who are facing the death of their brother or sister.

1. Adolescents as Comforters, Caregivers and Protectors for Parents.   Rosen (1986), in her book *Unspoken Grief,* confirms that society views loss and grief as being the most difficult for parents. At times, adolescents are expected to comfort, care for, and protect their parents. They are often considered to be old enough to be partners in bearing the burden of a dying child (Adams 1986). Sixteen-year-old Sarah, whose 7-year-old sister was dying of cancer, said:

> After all of this, maybe I'll be a good mother . . . I sure have had enough experience.

2. Adolescents as Partners, Friends, Confidants or Advisors.   In addition, these teens may be expected to act as partners, friends or confidants, especially to single parents, and be advisors concerning the status of their dying brother or sister. Linda said:

> I really didn't know how to help Mom make the decision to bring Tommy home . . . I wanted him to be at home but I was afraid that he might die and I wouldn't know what to do.

3. Adolescents as Baby-Sitters, Entertainers, and Caregivers for the Dying Child and Other Children.   A variety of roles may be imposed upon adolescent siblings by parents who understandably require help at such a difficult time. Such roles as babysitter, entertainer, and caregiver for the dying child and/or other children in the family may be expected. Joanne said:

> There were times when I just needed to get away . . . I wasn't lazy . . . I wanted to help look after Debbie, but I just couldn't handle her and the other kids too.

Adolescents' Vulnerability

Lazarus and Folkman (1984) noted that vulnerability is most often defined in terms of the adequacy of a person's resources. It is shaped by a combination of factors including personal capabilities, beliefs, and life commitments. People become vulnerable when what they value is put in jeopardy and their overall ability to cope on a daily basis is altered.

Factors Influencing Adolescent Vulnerability

The following factors may influence or alter adolescent siblings' perspectives of what is transpiring and may distort their abilities to cope, thus making them more vulnerable:

1. Stress of the Illness.   The emotional stress of cancer may severely alter the effectiveness of adolescents' coping abilities. Cancer still remains the commonest disease-related cause of childhood death. It brings a course of illness that illustrates almost every aspect of the struggle that families face when a child is dying from any lingering disease (Adams and Deveau 1986). The nature of this illness often creates a series of losses that set the stage for anticipatory grief. This adds to siblings' existing stress but does provide some conditioning and preparation for the actual death (Adams 1979; Adams and Deveau 1988).

At the beginning of palliative care, we often see the cumulative effects of the stress that began at the time of diagnosis. It has been well documented that siblings' vulnerability increases as the sick child's medical status declines (Sourkes 1981; Adams and Deveau 1987).

2. Anxiety Regarding Illness. Spinetta (1981) has noted that siblings' anxiety increases and remains elevated throughout the course of their brother's or sister's illness. Studies, including the work of Spinetta (1981) and of Cairns et al. (1979), have shown that the anxiety level in siblings of children with cancer is as high as, or higher than, the anxiety of siblings of children who have types of chronic long-term illnesses.

3. Anxiety Regarding the Whole Family. Unlike the dying child and their parents, siblings' anxiety tends to focus more on what has happened to the whole family and what will actually happen when the child dies (Spinetta 1981). Fifteen-year-old Tracey said:

> I didn't know things would change so much. I often wonder if we are going to get through this and how Mom and Dad will be after it is all over . . . Sometimes I wish it was all over . . . but then I'm afraid.

4. Identification with the Dying Child. When adolescents are facing the death of their sibling, they are exposed to the death of someone who is like themselves, who is part of their generation. They, therefore, are most vulnerable. Jason said:

> When Jim couldn't get up any more . . . I thought my life was over too . . . we had always done things together. . . .

5. Threat to Personal Integrity. For adolescent siblings, all that is stable, valued, and taken for granted is threatened (Adams and Deveau 1987). Sourkes (1981) states that increased pain and visible physical changes and distortions can be very distressing. Cairns et al. (1979) and Spinetta (1981) note that siblings may have negative body images that approximate those of the sick child. The impact of the impending death of their brother or sister can negatively affect their behavior and influence their reactions.

Feelings

No matter what the age of the dying child, adolescent siblings struggle with many of the following intense feelings in response to what is happening:

Sadness. Adolescents experience deep feelings of sadness and begin to rekindle or accelerate their process of anticipatory grief. They grieve for the dying child, for themselves, and for all of the changes and losses that their family has already incurred throughout the course of the illness. They suffer several losses including parental time, laughter and fun, important events, friends and relationships, and control over their lives. They know that life will not be the same again and ask, "Why must this happen at all?"

Anxiety. If you recall, I have already discussed anxiety in relation to the illness and the family as a factor in increased vulnerability. Now I would like to consider some of the issues that actually heighten this anxiety during palliative care.

Anxiety may be increased by fear of the child's death, fear of being alone with the child when the child dies, and fear of their own death or the death of their parents. There may also be anxiety concerning their own personal disintegration, that is, their ability not to fall apart during this crisis. In addition, adolescents may become anxious if there has been conflict between their parents during the course of the child's illness and if they are concerned about their parent(s)' distress and coping abilities during the terminal phase.

There will be increased anxiety if (a) the course of the illness and treatment has been very intensive and disruptive (Sourkes 1981); (b) if the physical decline of their brother or sister has been rapid or prolonged; (c) if there are many side effects including physical distortions; and (d) if the pain has been frequent and intense.

When children are dying in the hospital, anxiety may heighten as parents impose additional demands and responsibilities on adolescents who are expected to carry on at home (Adams and Deveau 1987, 1988). Terminal care at home with the family all together can be reassuring; however, it can augment any existing anxiety. If others become involved, the increased traffic flow tends to create a loss of privacy for the immediate family. Teens may benefit from the additional attention and help or they may lose attention as others dote upon the dying child. They may also feel inundated with adult company, values, and rituals (Adams and Deveau 1987).

> Tim, age 8, was dying at home. His mother was totally engrossed in his care, catered to his every need, and encouraged extended family to visit for long periods. Bill, his 14-year-old brother, could not stand the pressure—he retaliated against his mother and the situation by locking himself in his room at night and playing his drums.

Anger. Adolescents' anger may be provoked by many factors. Watching their brother or sister deteriorate or be in pain adds to their feelings of anger and helplessness. They may resent their parent(s) for their inability to protect their dying sibling and change the course of events. They may also be angry at God or the doctors for all of the trappings of the disease, the dying process, and the pain. Their anger may intensify as their hopes are dashed. They know that their sibling will not survive, that family life will not return to normal, and that their world will change permanently. These young people may struggle with anger that they direct at themselves for their ambivalence toward their dying sibling. They may resent their brother or sister for all of the changes that he or she is creating or has already created in the family. They may also feel anger toward their brother or sister for actually dying: "Why are you going to leave me alone?" "You were the only sister I could talk to . . . why do you have to die?"

When parents are distressed and have little control over their situation, they may try to establish controls in the form of rules and expectations of compliance over the lives of their other children. This may create animosity as well as isolation, especially for teens.

Guilt.   Guilt is a residual feeling that seldom has positive qualities; it may prevent siblings from expressing their difficult feelings and seeking the help and support that they require. Adolescent siblings may experience an increased awareness of personal feelings of responsibility and associated guilt if: (a) the dying child is resented for disrupting their lives; (b) they become the target for all of the dying child's anger; and (c) they feel that they did not protect their brother or sister from dying (Sourkes 1981; Adams and Deveau, 1987). If they were transplant donors and the procedure was unsuccessful, their guilt may be overwhelming because they feel responsible for not saving their sibling and for letting everyone down. Actions such as arguing, ignoring demands, or telling off their dying sibling may further compound their guilt. Taking time out to get away or to have some fun with friends may create difficult feelings later on. Monica expressed her guilt as follows:

> I really wanted to go to that rock concert, but I felt so awful after I came home and found that Michelle was much worse.

They may also feel guilty for being healthy: "Dad's only son is dying, I should be the one to die."

Jealousy.   Jealousy is especially evident when adolescents are close in age to the dying child (Bank and Kahn 1982). There may be jealousy because of the special favors, allowances, and attention granted the dying child by parents and relatives. If teens believe that their brother or sister has caused their parents to reject or abandon them, their feelings of resentment may deepen.

Rejection.   When the world seems to revolve around the dying child, siblings may be unable to find emotional support at home and feel rejected. Sourkes (1981) notes that adolescent siblings view their parents as being more distant and their families as having less cohesion. Rejected siblings feel very uncertain about themselves and their capabilities. Their feelings of inferiority often become visible in peer relationships and at school (Adams and Deveau 1987). Teens may also mistake the natural phenomenon of distancing prior to death as a form of rejection by their dying brother or sister.

Loneliness and Isolation.   Parents who are coping with a dying child frequently feel an overwhelming sense of isolation. If adolescent siblings are cast in the role of caregiver, their feelings of isolation may also be overwhelming because they need a social life outside of the home. If the child is dying in hospital and these siblings are overburdened with household responsibilities, parental absences can create extreme feelings of loneliness as well as isolation from what is happening (Adams and Deveau 1987). In single parent families, adolescents may feel very lonely and isolated in their role as comforter both for the dying child and the parent. Where is their guidance and support?

Adults often assume that these young people do not want us to intrude on their privacy and therefore, we do not provide them with the support that they need. Rosen (1986) points out that the majority of adults who were bereaved adolescent siblings did not share their feelings with anyone and felt isolated and rejected. One teen said: "No one else is experiencing what is happening to my family, so no one can really understand me."

With the focus on the dying child, adolescents' plans may change or be postponed in order to accommodate the demands of the crisis at hand. College, travel, or career opportunities may be discouraged by parents and relatives. Parents may rationalize that, unlike the dying child, healthy siblings will be here tomorrow. On the other hand, teens may delay or change their plans because they feel obligated to help out:

> Eighteen-year-old Sharon had been accepted into university. However, her parents
> silence and lack of support for her to move away strongly influenced her decision
> to remain at home to help care for her dying sister and her two younger siblings.

Coping Mechanisms and Responses Common to Adolescent Siblings

It is against adolescents' very nature to accept death without contention (Adams and Deveau 1986). The intensity of the feelings that these teens experience leads them to use many of the following defense mechanisms in order to cope and to protect themselves:

Denial.   Denial of what is happening and the probable final outcome is not uncommon. It fulfills a need for self-survival—a chance to rest from reality, regenerate strength, and gather energy to carry on.

Avoidance/Withdrawal. Withdrawal or avoidance also provides temporary escape. The reality of dying may bring on a natural withdrawal. Older adolescents may retreat into themselves and become preoccupied with the meanings of life and death, perhaps preparing for or rehearsing the actual death of their sibling in their dreams. In an attempt to cope with the stress and frustrations at home, teens may try to: (a) avoid any confrontation with their parents that will force them to deal with the difficulties at hand; (b) seek refuge in their peer group; or (c) escape into a world of drugs and alcohol (Adams and Deveau 1987).

Compensation. Adolescents who experience feelings of inadequacy and inferiority may also withdraw into their peer group and use drugs and alcohol in an attempt to compensate for their poor self image.

Projection. When adolescent siblings are faced with the anger of a dying brother or sister the impact can be devastating, especially when they were trying to be helpful (Sourkes 1981). Because it is not acceptable to be overtly angry with a dying child, these teens may project their anger and frustration onto their parents, peers, or other significant people in their lives.

> Ken, who was usually an easy going 13 year old, gradually became irritable and demanding with his teacher. As his brother's condition deteriorated, he isolated himself from classmates and would pick fights in gym class and the school yard.

Somatization. If emotions cannot be expressed or resolved, there is a tendency for some teens to internalize their anxiety through their own physical symptoms. Headaches, stomach pains, and insomnia are common. Some siblings may actually emulate the physical symptoms of their dying brother or sister. This is especially common in siblings that have very close relationships with each other (Cain, Fast and Erickson 1964; Binger et al. 1969; Bank and Kahn 1982).

Regression. Regression is usually precipitated by severe stress. Teens who become overwhelmed may revert back to behavior that was common at an earlier stage of their development. Irritability, unreasonable demands, and tantrums may be typical reactions. Though these behaviors meet their need for attention, they do go against their need for independence and the freedom to make their own choices and decisions (Adams and Deveau 1987).

Control/Mastery. And finally, a positive coping response is the ability to gain control or mastery of their situation. The need for control goes beyond their desire for independence and is closely linked to their need to temper their anxiety (Adams and Deveau 1986). In an attempt to gain control over the situation, adolescents may do the following: (a) gain knowledge about the disease and what to expect through reading and asking questions of the physician and their parents; (b) insist that they be a part of the decision making concerning their brother's or sister's care; and (c) assume an active role in helping out.

When teens help out they are attempting to fulfill the following needs: (a) to be a part of the family; (b) to identify with their parents; (c) to show that they care; and (d) to compensate for their frustration and anger (Adams and Deveau 1987).

For some adolescents, another means of gaining control is to join a religious group or other similar organization. Such involvement may provide emotional support, understanding, and respite.

Factors Influencing Siblings' Adjustment to the Impending Death of their Brother or Sister

After studying the literature on sibling grief, I believe that the following factors are important in siblings' adjustment to the death of their brother or sister and to bereavement:

1. Parent and family communication patterns—the more open the communication, the better children will adapt (Spinetta 1981; Coleman and Coleman 1984);
2. The amount of emotional support provided within the family;
3. Siblings' ability to understand the disease and the dying process;
4. Siblings' relationship with the dying child; and
5. Siblings' degree of involvement in the care of the dying child. In a study by Lauer et al. (1985), siblings felt that their *own involvement in the care* of their dying brother or sister was the *most important aspect* of their experience.

Poor Sibling Adjustment

The adjustment of siblings is closely related to their parents' ability to cope and to the level of support that they receive. Davies (1987) noted that siblings who have the most difficulties after a brother or sister dies tend to come from families that:

a) are not well integrated;
b) provide limited support;
c) are in conflict;
d) have difficulties communicating with each other;

e) have lower levels of parental education and income;

f) lack clear moral and religious practices; and

g) have little emphasis on participating together in social and recreational activities.

From this we can conclude that if siblings are left out at a time when the family needs to pull together, then they will be left out during bereavement. If they receive little or no support during the time of impending death they will probably not receive support later. If the communication pattern is poor throughout the course of the child's illness, it is unlikely to change during palliative care without major intervention.

Reactions to Grief: Positive Implications

There is no question that having a brother or sister who is dying creates tremendous stress in the life of adolescent siblings. Though coping is difficult, it is not beyond the capabilities of many of these teens. They do find ways to come to terms with their situation and cope with the additional anxiety and responsibilities. Davies (1987) found that 75 percent of all siblings do well after such a death. She states that these teens frequently acquire an increased sense of responsibility and confidence at ages 13 to 16 years. They tend to mature earlier and to develop a greater capacity for empathy. They appreciate life differently and seem to gain more from each day. The warmth and concern shown by parents, family members, and caregivers, can provide adolescents with role models for becoming genuinely helpful people. It may also provide them with a framework for career definition as many lean toward the helping professions (Adams and Deveau 1987). Those who do survive the death of their brother or sister also acquire skills that may help them to cope with the challenges and responsibilities that they may encounter as adults.

Conclusion

Adolescent siblings who must face the death of their brother or sister are very vulnerable because they are confronted with a tragic experience that is emotionally demanding and draining and will have lasting effects. As professionals, we need to understand their stage of development, recognize their needs, and be sensitive to their coping responses. In closing, I would like to leave you with the following guidelines:

1. We must acknowledge the unique bonds between siblings.

2. We should avoid stereotyping adolescents. Try to meet them at their own level and deal with them as individuals, with specific feelings and

needs, rather than projecting or imposing your own expectations and perceptions. Do not expect them to feel as you do.

3. Parents and caregivers need to be honest and communicate openly with teens. Information concerning the progress of the illness, possible changes, and prognosis should be shared with them.

4. Include adolescent siblings in the discussions and decision making concerning their dying brother's or sister's care.

5. Encourage parents and adolescent siblings to discuss and agree upon reasonable expectations and responsibilities.

6. Provide these teens with the opportunity to negotiate their own degree of involvement during terminal care and support their decisions.

7. Recognize and show appreciation for their efforts to help out and to assume additional responsibilities.

8. Provide support and reassurance on a continuing basis and especially during terminal care and bereavement. Where available, encourage teens to join sibling support groups and attend summer and winter camps.

9. Recognize that adolescent siblings need to go on living. They need their own time, their own space, access to peers, and opportunities to maintain their own life outside of their family.

References

Adams, D. W. 1979. *Childhood malignancy: The psychosocial care of the child and his family.* Springfield, IL: C. C. Thomas.

——1984. Helping the dying child: Practical approaches for non-physicians. In H. Wass and C. A. Corr, eds. *Childhood and death.* Washington, DC: Hemisphere, pp. 95–112.

—— 1986. Understanding sibling grief and helping siblings to cope. In G. H. Paterson, ed. *Children and death.* London, Ontario: King's College, pp. 35–42.

Adams, D. W. and E. J. Deveau 1986. Helping dying adolescents: Needs and responses. In C. A. Corr and J. N. McNeil, eds. *Adolescence and death.* New York: Springer, pp. 79–96.

—— 1987. How the cause of a child's death may affect a sibling's grief. In M. A. Morgan, ed. *Bereavement: Helping the survivors.* London, Ontario: King's College, pp. 67–78.

——1987. When a brother or sister is dying of cancer: The vulnerability of the adolescent sibling. *Death Studies* 11:279–85.

——1988. *Coping with childhood cancer: Where do we go from here?* Hamilton, Ontario: Kinbridge.

Attig, T. 1986. Death themes in adolescent music: The classic years. In C. A. Corr and J. N. McNeil, eds. *Adolescence and death.* New York: Springer, pp. 32–56.

Bank, S. P. and M. D. Kahn. 1982. *The sibling bond.* New York: Basic Books.

Binger, C. M., A. R. Ablin, R. C. Feuerstein, J. H. Kushner, S. Zoger and C. Mikkelsen. 1969. Childhood leukemia: Emotional impact on patient and family. *New England Journal of Medicine* 280:414–18.

Breslau, N. 1982. Siblings of disabled children: Birth order and age spacing effects. *Journal of Abnormal Child Psychology* 10: 85–96.

Cain, A. C. I. Fast, and M. E. Erickson. 1964. Children's disturbed reactions to the death of sibling. *American Journal of Orthopsychiatry* 34:741–52.

Cairns, N. U., G. M. Clark, S. D. Smith and S. B. Lansky. 1979. Adaptation of siblings to childhood malignancy. *The Journal of Pediatrics* 95: 484–87.

Coleman, F. W. and W. Coleman. 1984. Helping siblings and other peers cope with dying. In H. Wass and C. A. Corr, eds. *Childhood and death.* Washington, DC: Hemisphere, pp. 129–47.

Corr, C. A. and J. N. McNeil. 1986. Adolescence and death: Contemporary interactions. In C. A. Corr and J. N. McNeil, eds. *Adolescence and death.* New York: Springer, pp. 1–3.

Davies, E. 1987. After a child dies. In M. A. Morgan, ed. *Bereavement: Helping the survivors* London, Ontario: King's College, pp. 55–66.

Drotar, D. 1978. Adaptational problems of children and adolescents with cystic fibrosis. *Journal of Pediatric Psychiatry* 3:45.

Fleming, S. J. and R. Adolph. 1986. Helping bereaved adolescents: Needs and responses. In C. A. Corr & J. N. McNeil, eds. *Adolescence and death.* New York: Springer, pp. 97–118.

Furman, W. and D. Burhmester. 1985. Children's perceptions of the qualities of sibling relationships. *Child Development* 56:448–61.

Gordon, A. K. 1986. The tattered cloak of immortality. In C. A. Corr and J. N. McNeil, eds. *Adolescence and death.* New York: Springer, pp. 16–31.

Lauer, M., R. Mulhern, J. Bohne and B. Camitta 1985. Children's perceptions of their sibling's death at home or hospital: The precursors of differential adjustment. *Cancer Nursing* February: 21–27.

Lazarus, R. S. and S. Folkman. 1984. *Stress appraisal and coping.* New York: Springer, pp. 50–51.

Lewis, M. 1982. *Clinical aspects of child development.* Philadelphia: Lea & Febiger, pp. 263–341.

Minuchin, S. 1974. *Families and family therapy.* Cambridge, MA: Harvard University Press.

Osterweiss, M. 1986. Developmental and long range sequelae of childhood loss. Paper presented at Sixth World Congress on the Care of the Terminally Ill, September 27, Montreal, Quebec.

Penn, P. 1983. Coalitions and binding interactions in families with chronic illness. *Family systems Medicine* 1:6–25.

Rosen, A. 1986. *Unspoken grief.* Lexington, KY: D.C. Heath.

Siemon, M. 1984. Siblings of the chronically ill or disabled child. *Nursing Clinics of North America* 19: 295–307.

Sourkes, B. 1981. Siblings of the pediatric cancer patient. In J. Kellerman, ed. *Psychological aspects of childhood cancer.* Springfield, IL: Charles C. Thomas, pp. 47–69.

Spinetta, J. J. 1981. The sibling of the child with cancer. In J. J. Spinetta and P. Deasy-Spinetta, eds. *Living with childhood cancer* St. Louis, MO: C. V. Mosby, pp. 133–42.

8

Long-term Follow-up of Bereaved Siblings

Betty Davies, RN, PhD

I would like to begin by telling you the story of a woman named Amanda Jones. Her story represents the story of many siblings who, in their childhood, had a brother or sister die. Amanda was eight years old when diphtheria spread through her small town in rural Saskatchewan. The disease claimed the lives of both her brother and sister, who were seven and nine years of age. Amanda vividly remembers several scenes. She remembers a long ladder being placed against the wall of her tall, two-storey house, just barely reaching the upstairs window of the sick room where the ill children were being cared for. She remembers seeing the body of her brother being lifted through the window, carried cautiously down the ladder and taken away for instant burial. Spreading the disease by carrying the body through the house could not be risked and there was no time for funerals because the bodies of diphtheria victims had to be destroyed quickly. Amanda's house was quarantined and she was not allowed beyond her front door. But as a child of eight, Amanda found the confinement boring. And on the eventful day, the adults seemed particularly upset. Amanda became restless and sneaked out the front door to seek solace in the shade of her favorite tree at the side of the house. Through its branches Amanda alone witnessed her brother's last journey. She knew he had died, not because anyone had told her, but because she "just knew." Two days later the view through the branches was repeated. This time her sister's body became the second bundle to leave via the precarious ladder. Amanda stood watching in silence, wondering why they had to die, especially her brother. They had been so close, lying together and sharing secrets from their two older sisters.

No one spoke to Amanda about what had happened, no one explained what this terrible disease really was. Even her older sister, who usually talked about everybody, would not talk about her brother or sister. Amanda sensed that her mother was very distressed; she wasn't sure about her father though because he didn't cry and he told everyone else not to cry because "it wouldn't help anyway." Without any explanations or discussions about what had happened, Amanda developed her own theory. "There must a be reason why I survived and they didn't," thought the young child, "Especially since we were in the same family and all. That awful disease didn't get me so there must be something special about my life. I will have to be very special."

Amanda was an average student in school, even though she worked very hard to attain good grades. She grew up experiencing many of the trials and tribulations that all young women experience, though she faced them alone. She had a quiet social life, preferring to spend her time reading or walking alone among her trees. She searched continuously for something special. Amanda did not have the opportunity to study beyond high school, which she regretted because she wanted to study to be someone special.

As a young adult, Amanda married a "nice fellow," a plumber. Within a few years, she had several youngsters of her own, all of whom developed into average students in school. Amanda devoted all of her efforts to being a good mother. Consequently, she did not have time to develop many friendships of her own, though she was always willing to offer helping hands to others in trouble. Death did not frighten Amanda in any way so she did not shy away from tragedy. As her children grew and left home to take on regular jobs and to begin families of their own, Amanda sensed a growing anxiety inside. At age 55, the anxiety became too much to bear and she experienced an emotional breakdown.

With therapy, Amanda learned about her hidden self. She reviewed her earlier theory that had guided, unconsciously, every aspect of her life: "That awful disease didn't get me, so there must be something special about my life. I will have to be very special." At 55, Amanda did not see herself as very special at all, even though, "God knows I tried." She did not have a career, a profession, a job of her own. For women of her generation, this was not unusual, but to Amanda, it meant that she had failed. Her marriage was solid and satisfying in many ways, but her husband was an average man; no great accomplishments were among his possessions. Again, Amanda perceived personal failure—she had failed in choosing a special man. Though she had given her heart and soul to motherhood, she felt a failure in this realm too. Her children had not attained scholastic excellence, nor had they won any awards or pursued professional careers. Now they were married and were having their own ordinary children, just as she had done. Where had she gone astray? How had she betrayed her reason for surviving?

While in therapy, Amanda shared the story of the diphtheria deaths. She remembers, word for word, the psychiatrist's response: "You know, Amanda, diseases like diphtheria strike individuals only by chance. Your brother and sister got diphtheria by chance, you did not get diphtheria by chance. That's all it means. That's how those things happen." His words touched Amanda, "deep within my core. It was like lifting a heavy cloak from weary shoulders for the first time. For the first time since I was eight years old I knew why my brother and sister had died and why I had survived. I cannot tell you what a feeling that was."

"Even now," said Amanda during our interview, "I still must make an effort to remember those words. It's hard to change your way of looking at the world, but I've done it. My husband and kids have helped a lot and my life has been much better since that breakdown. Those deaths are still with me but in a different way now." When Amanda told me her story she was 75 years old.

Amanda Jones' story illustrates many aspects of the siblings' long-term experience following the death of a brother or sister. In this chapter I will elaborate on several of these aspects, using information derived from several sets of data.

The experience of bereavement has received relatively little attention as a concept and almost no attention as an experience to be researched. This is particularly true for sibling bereavement. While it is recognized that the death of a parent is indeed a traumatic event for a young child, potentially leading to long-term effects, the death of a sibling has not been viewed in the same way. There have been several studies of the effects on children of experiencing parental death; however, relatively little research has been reported in the area of sibling bereavement. My first study was conducted with 34 families in which a child had died from cancer up to three years before the data were obtained, and in which there was at least one other child between 6 and 16 years of age. The overall purpose of this study was to examine the behavioral responses of the children to the death of their sibling and to examine these in relation to selected variables: individual, situational, and environmental. Individual variables included age and sex of both the surviving and deceased children. Situational variables were duration of illness, (how long the ill child had been sick before he died), the type of cancer, and the time that had elapsed since the death. Finally, I included several environmental variables that my clinical experience suggested were of importance to bereavement outcome in children. These variables were sibling closeness, sibling involvement, and family environment. The majority of the deceased children were male (23), ranging in age from 1 to 19 years at the time of their death. The average number of surviving children in the family was 2.5; however, for the purpose of the initial analysis, only one child in each family was included, that is, 34 children. The second analysis was completed for all surviving children. Fifty-five children comprised this data set. The third data set derived from 58 families in the midwestern United States who participated in a home care program for dying children that was developed by Dr. Ida Martinson. These families had been assessed at periodic intervals since the death of a child, most recently at seven to nine years after the death. I had the good fortune of doing post-doctoral study with Dr. Martinson and it was during that time that I had access to her data. My analysis focused on the sibling data. The fourth study is one that I am currently conducting. It involves interviewing adults who, in their childhood, lost a sibling. The previous studies were limited to families where a child had died from cancer; this last study includes individuals whose sibling died from a variety of causes.[1]

Subjects

The 34 families who comprised the first studies resided in geographic areas within both the United States and Canada, specifically in Washington, Arizona, and Alberta. The majority (30) of the families were two-parent families. Parents' mean age was 39.5 years; they were all Caucasian and most were of a Protestant faith. Most had at least some college education and they were employed in a wide range of occupations. Families were obtained from several sources including two Pediatric/Haematology/Oncology clinics, the private practice of a Pediatric Oncologist, and a chapter of Candlelighters (a support group for parents of children with cancer).

Of the 34 surviving children who comprised the first sibling sample, over three-fifths (21) were female and the rest (13) were male. Fourteen were in the school-age category (6 to 11 years) and 20 were young adolescents (12 to 16 years). My original goal had been to study young children, particularly those between 6 and 11 years of age, but it was difficult to find enough children of that age group. Consequently, I had to expand it to include children between the ages of 6 and 16. Of the 55 siblings who comprised the second group, 34 were female and 21 were male. Twenty-three fell into the school-age category and 27 were adolescents. There were a total of 71 siblings in the families who participated in the third study. Their mean age was 18.7 years and included those children who had been born or adopted since the child's death. In the current study, seven subjects have been interviewed thus far. They range in age from 25 to 75 years. They experienced the death of a sibling in their childhood, that is, before their seventeenth birthday.

Procedures

All of the studies utilized interviews with the subjects, including the siblings themselves, which is unusual since much of the work that has been done with

1. Without the support of several granting agencies these studies would not have been possible. The National Health and Research Development Program in Ottawa financed the first study; the Alberta Foundation for Nursing Research funded the second; the California Division of the American Cancer Society funded the third; and the fourth is being funded by a new faculty grant at the University of British Columbia.

siblings talks to parents about the siblings rather than talking to the siblings. In addition, several objective assessments were completed with the siblings: I will refer to those only as necessary as I present my conclusions.

Results

I have selected certain results to share on the basis of the findings from the various studies, which support several broader conclusions that I have made about the experience of long-term sibling bereavement. The process of data collection and analysis is ongoing; my goal is to explicate clearly my theory about sibling bereavement.

Four positive aspects of the long-term effects of experiencing the death of a sibling have been identified in all studies. Amanda Jones said that she was able to face death as a result of her experience. Death was not something that frightened or worried her, at least not her own death. However, she did remember worrying about her own children dying, especially when they were the same age as her brother and sister had been when they succumbed to diphtheria. In the seven- to nine-year study, continuing concerns about the recurrence of cancer in themselves or in other family members were common among the surviving siblings. Alterations in health status were reasons for concern; some even worried that younger siblings had been born with cancer or expressed concern for their own future offspring. These concerns were also expressed by the siblings in the three-year study. However, the majority of siblings in all studies felt as Amanda did. Their encounter with death enabled them to feel somewhat comfortable with death—at least they were able to face it instead of avoiding it. It was this ability that allowed them to help others who were experiencing death: "I think his death has made me able to deal with other people and with people dying. I've had a couple of friends talk to me and ask for my help because they had a brother or sister or father or mother that died and they know that I had too." Encountering death also contributed to the siblings' view of life in a constructive way. They felt that they gained an understanding of the meaning of life in a way that they would not have gained otherwise. They valued life, realizing that it is only a temporary gift. One 16-year-old boy commented, "I have a better outlook on life now. I mean, I realize how important life is as a result of my sister's death."

Feeling comfortable with death, being able to help others, and developing a sensitive outlook on life contributed to a fourth positive outcome: feeling good about oneself. This was an aspect I was particularly interested in; data from the three-year study indicated that the children who were adapting best were those who seemed to be doing well in many aspects of their lives and generally feeling good about themselves. Self-concept was assessed in the seven- to nine-year study. The question that guided the analysis was: What is the effect, if any, on the self-concept of children whose sibling died from cancer? The Piers-Harris *Self-Concept Scale for Children* was the instrument used to assess self-concept. This scale is quickly completed by the children themselves and is designed for children between the ages of 8 and 18 years. It consists of eighty first-person statements that simply require a Yes or No response. It is judged to have good internal consistency and adequate temporal stability. As I said earlier, there were 71 siblings in the 58 families. Of these siblings, 29 were between 8 and 18 years of age, the appropriate age for this particular instrument. Their average age was 14.17 and there were ten males and nineteen females. In exploring this particular aspect, I found that indeed the bereaved children as a group scored higher than the norms predicted. From adversity had come an impetus for psychological growth, reflected in the overall higher self-concept scores.

For some of the siblings, their new view of life resulting from their encounter with death had a shadow side as well. This aspect was less of an impetus for growth but rather tended to stifle their growth, in particular their social growth. They had come to see life as very precious, but for many, with the new found maturity came a seriousness about life and about what was important in life. Like Amanda, their outlook became a "heavy cloak weighing down weary shoulders." There was no room for the normal developmental antics of childhood and adolescence. For such siblings, the carryings-on of their peers were intolerable. Their friends' behavior and interests became trivial. Unable to shed the cloak of responsibility, these siblings withdrew from their previous involvements. They dropped out of Scouts, team sports and weekend parties. Instead, they chose to be alone or they occasionally joined the company of selected adults who seemed to share their world view. In exchange for their new maturity, they sacrificed the frivolity of childhood. Not only that, they seemed to be paying continuous installments on a never-ending debt of loneliness.

At this point, I want to refer specifically to one aspect of the three-year study. One of the purposes of this study was to examine the behavioral responses of the bereaved siblings. To do this, I used an objective measure of children's behavior called the Achenbach *Child Behaviour Checklist*. It obtains parents reports of both behavior problems and competencies in their 4- to 16-year-old children in a standardized format. Standardized norms are provided for children according to age and sex. This instrument is reported to demonstrate face and construct validity and test-retest reliability. Summary scores in four areas were used for analysis: Total Behavior Problem Scores; Total Internalizing Scores (that is, problems within the self, such as "withdrawn"); Total Externalizing Scores (problems with the outside world, such as "aggressive"); and Total Social Competence Sores. (the child's school performance and the amount and quality of his or her participation in sports, hobbies, chores, and other social relationships). The children's internalizing behavior problem scores were higher than predicted from the norms, and their social competency scores were less than predicted from the norms. Furthermore, there was a negative relationship between social competency and time elapsed since the death; that is, the siblings became less socially competent over time.

At the time of death, normal grief responses include withdrawing kinds of behaviors. People do not necessarily want contact with others, or they feel ambivalent about who they want to be with. They may not want to be alone but they find socializing difficult. It takes a while to even begin to resume one's former activities. This was the same for the children in the study.

Given the kinds of behaviors that are defined as internalizing then, it is not surprising that they occurred frequently since they are closely related to normal grief responses. Decreased participation in activities and decreased social interaction have been reported as part of normal grief responses. Such alterations would account for the decreased participation of bereaved children in activities and in their relationships with friends. Further, since school attendance is a major daily activity of 6- to 16-year-old children, it can be expected that decreased school performance may also result for the same reasons. Of particular interest, however, is the finding that 50 percent of the bereaved children were reported to be sad. But, again, sadness is a normal concomitant of grief. Few references, however, indicate that sadness lasts for as long as three years. These findings suggest that long lasting sadness may be an outcome of bereavement in siblings that occurs with greater frequency than the literature indicates.

"Lonely" and "likes to be alone" were two other behaviors reported for almost 50 percent of the children. These behaviors are also considered part of normal grief. But, again, remember that these behaviors were being reported up to three years after the death. Remember also that when the relationships between variables were examined, there was a negative correlation between the social competence scores and the time elapsed since the death. That is, the longer the time since the death, the less socially competent the children became.

In the study looking at the siblings seven to nine years after the death of their brother or sister, many of these siblings report similar behaviors. Nearly all siblings indicated that at the time of death, sadness, feeling depressed, and feeling lonely had been big problems and they reported that these problems continued. Mark, for example, nine years after the death of his sister said, "She was my only sister and after she died I was so lonely. The loneliness was the hardest thing; it still is, you know, and I still get depressed sometimes."

The next question then was: Are these behaviors indicative of disturbed reactions in the children? To begin to answer this question, I compared the percentages of behavior problems in the bereaved children with the percentages that Achenbach provides for referred and nonreferred children. Referred children were those under the care of child mental health professionals and nonreferred children were those not receiving such care. The rates of occurrence for "Unhappy, sad, or depressed" and for "Lonely" were within the range of occurrence for referred children. "Likes to be alone" fell close to the upper end of the range for nonreferred children. The point is that the frequencies of these behaviors for children up to three years after the death of their sibling, were more like those for referred children than for normal or nonreferred children. Furthermore, about 25 percent of the bereaved children demonstrated behavior problems to a degree that was indicative of possible psychopathology. The authors of the CBCL indicate that only 10 percent of the normal population of children the same age and sex would be expected to demonstrate these behaviors. Therefore, it seems that bereaved children demonstrate many behaviors that might be considered manifestations of normal grief: sadness, withdrawal, and loneliness. However, about one of every four siblings demonstrate these behaviors to such a degree that we should be sensitive to the behaviors as indicative of possible psychopathology. Furthermore, these behaviors can and do last for a very long time.

Another question arises: When do the normal grief behaviors become detrimental to the development of the sibling? The normal grief behaviors serve a protective function, guarding the vulnerable self until the individual is ready, once again, to face the world. It seems with siblings, though, that the sadness and withdrawal of normal grief are compounded by the sense of isolation that they feel due to their new view of the world. Instead of being able to turn to their peers for support, for understanding, they withdraw from them because they find their interests and behavior trivial. Grieving adults often do this too. But the difference is that adults, on the whole, have already accomplished the developmental tasks of earlier years. The bereaved children have not. As a result, their withdrawal removes them from the world of friendship and fun and from the normal experience of growing up with peers. These siblings tend to miss out on learning how to get along with same-age friends. They miss out on learning appropriate social skills. This in turn contributes to their loneliness and sadness and their sense of isolation, and these behaviors become on-going and may last a lifetime.

Conclusions

This is a part of newly developing theory and I have yet to work out all of the dimensions. I do have a few ideas from my data that provide clues as to what enables siblings to respond to the death in the least detrimental way. One clue comes from the self-concept analysis. Though as a group the self-concept scores of the children were considerably higher than the norms, within the group there was a considerable range of scores. I was interested in finding out what might contribute to optimal levels of self-concept. I analyzed the sibling and parent interview data for the siblings who had the highest scores and for those who had the lowest. The children in the lowest group shared one common characteristic: they felt as though they were "not enough." Feelings of not being "enough" came about through several means. They were compared unfavorably to the deceased child, they somehow felt responsible for the death, or they did not feel special within the family. Being compared unfavorably with the sibling had not necessarily happened since the death of the child, but occurred even before the child had become ill. One little girl, for example, described her grandmother's long-standing favoritism toward the deceased sibling: "When it was Paul's birthday, she would send Paul a present. When it was my birthday she would send me a present, but she'd also send Paul a present. She always told me, why can't you be a good person just like your brother, Paul." Second, they felt displaced by the addition of new children to the family. "If I were enough," they would reason, "then why is it that Mom and Dad need more kids?" Consequently, the siblings' environment had much to do with their long-term response. Data from the first and second studies indicate this to be so as well. Here, the Moos *Family Environment Scale* was used to measure various aspects of the family environment, which refers to the social climate within families. This instrument is a 90-item true-false questionnaire that focuses on the measurement and descriptions of various aspects of family social climate, as portrayed by 10 subscales. Results pertaining to the relationships between the children's behavior and characteristics of their family environments indicated several significant findings. Both externalizing and internalizing behaviors negatively related to cohesion in the families. That is, the greater the feeling of closeness among family members, the fewer behavior problems there were in the children.

What seems to be important in these studies was the communication the bereaved children received about themselves, about their deceased sibling, and about the events as they were happening. Including children in events, explaining to them what is happening, and reassuring them about their role in the situation and in the family are critical. This communication, however, may not have to come directly from the parents who are, of course, overstressed as it is. It may come from others who are close to the children, from grandparents, family friends or other members of the family support system. Data from the *FES* suggest that social support is important to siblings' bereavement outcome. For example, Sarah was 16 years old. Her family had moved from the east coast to their new home in the west because of her father's unemployment and he was searching for new work. For a while they lived in an upstairs apartment in a house. They then moved to their own townhouse but said, "We don't have much to do with the folks here." When their son died, they found a minister by looking through the yellow pages. "We don't have family, it's just us." At the funeral, only the three of them attended. But the mother said, "I can't really remember if any of Sarah's friends were there or not." Sarah, at 16, was the only child in the entire study who had actually dropped out of school. Her scores on the behavior problems scales were at the 97th percentile. Her social competence score was at less than the 4th percentile. Her family's scores on the measures called the Intellectual, Cultural Orientation, and the Moral/Religious Emphasis were two and three, respectively. The highest score on these scales could be a nine. In contrast, was 14-year-old David's family. His mother said,

> For a year after Rhonda's death we were not alone on any one night. My nephew who had lost his brother, he understood, he came to stay. He was twenty-two and he came to tidy up the yard and help around the house and be with the boys. During the whole time of Rhonda's final illness, my brother, he's a priest, was here. My elderly aunt came too. Everyone was at the funeral, the boys' friends from school and scouts and their teachers and even my teachers because they knew Rhonda from a project I had done about her.

In contrast to Sarah, David's scores on the problem behavior checklists were at the 10th percentile. His social competence scores were at the 90th percentile and his family's scores on the measures of social involvement were as high as they could be (9). The families with the highest scores on the subscales of Intellectual, Cultural Orientation, Active/ Recreational Orientation, and Moral/ Religious Emphasis had children with the lowest internalizing behavior problems and the highest social competence scores. An emphasis on these values may predispose the families to participate in recreational, cultural, social and religious activities or events, thereby increasing the likelihood of social involvement, which in turn may promote adaptive behaviors in the children. In families with greater social involvements, the more likely it is that the children will have someone available to meet their needs.

To summarize, my argument is this: The death of a brother or sister is a traumatic event resulting in a variety of reactions that most often include internalizing behavior such as sadness, loneliness, and social withdrawal. These are manifestations of normal grief. Altered views of life and its meaning are also common outcomes of grief. In children and adolescents, however, this new view may contribute to a sense of isolation. In an environment where siblings are not given explanations about the situation, reassurances about their responses and their special value, or opportunities to share in the grief of the whole family, these reactions can potentially become lifelong patterns of behavior—at least they may last until intervention is sought. I want to conclude now with the story of Susan: listen for the variables and how they interacted for her.

> Susan was 13 years old when her brother, Martin, turned on the car in the closed garage and gave his life to carbon monoxide poisoning. On the eventful day, Susan was changing buses on her way home from her weekly dancing lesson when she

ran into her sister and so they walked home together. Susan was never very close to 18-year-old Mary and they didn't have much to say as they walked toward their house. Consequently, Susan had no hesitation in leaving her sister behind to run ahead when she saw the car of her favorite family friends in front of the house. They did not come to visit very often, but Susan was so glad to see them whenever they did. Susan's dad met her in the driveway with the words, "Martin is dead." Susan pushed him away and laughed. Susan didn't like her dad; he was a violent man and neither she nor any of her brothers or sisters ever talked to him about anything. In fact, Susan spent most of her time trying to avoid him. She ran to the steps, there seeing her mother in tears. At that moment Susan knew her father's words were true. Feeling very mixed up and wanting to cry and not being able to, Susan stood dazed. Her father told her that wasn't the way to act at a time like this. She shouldn't try to cry just because she thought that was the thing to do. Susan was mystified . . . she didn't even know how she felt, let alone thinking about "behaving as she was supposed to." Like Amanda, Susan received no explanations. She was only able to piece together the story on her own by overhearing little bits of conversations. No one talked to Susan about her brother, his death, or about how she, Susan, was feeling or about what she was thinking. Somehow, she and her reactions didn't seem important. When she did cry she was scolded. One day Susan found her mother crying. "Why is it O.K. for you to cry?" she asked. "Because I have lost my son, you've only lost your brother," came the sorrowful reply.

Susan was very sad and lonely. Martin had been her favorite brother. He was four years older than she and was protective of his little sister. She remembers how he had taken her skiing, showing her how to use the edges to turn properly. Before his death, Susan had been an active, outgoing person at school but since his death Susan hadn't felt like doing much, choosing instead to stay home, playing table games with her aunt, a nun, who had come to visit for a short while. Her friends missed her though, and called her out for pizza. "It all seemed so silly," said Susan, "how could they spend hours talking and giggling about all that dumb fashion stuff when clothes weren't all that important compared to what happened to Martin." Susan didn't accept their invitations and soon they stopped coming. She preferred the quiet solitude of her books. Susan continued to feel very lonely and she missed her brother terribly. But no one seemed to understand. Of course, how could they? No one in the family ever talked about Martin, so how could she share her thoughts with them? Besides, they were all too busy with their own lives. Mary and her other brother were such problem kids that they got all the attention. Schoolmates were no help either; Susan didn't really associate with them. At 21, on top of heavy university courses, the sadness and loneliness were too much for Susan. She sought the help of a psychiatrist. With his help, Susan began to come out from under her heavy cloak. At 23, she developed some new friendships among theater people: "They were the only ones who just accepted me for what I was." Now 25, Susan says, "I have a BA and a resume that shows I have absolutely no work experience. I feel like I'm really only 19 or so. You see, I lost the years between 13 and 21 and now I have to catch up somehow.'' At least Susan didn't have to wait until she was 55 as Amanda had done.

Sibling bereavement has received relatively little attention until recent years. The goal of my research has been to document the long-term effects of sibling bereavement and to identify those factors which influence these effects. This work is nearly done and will, I hope, serve as a basis for an intervention program for siblings. I believe that through the interrelated processes of research and theory development and intervention, we can do much to promote the optimal development of young children whose brother or sister has died. With appropriate intervention we can help bereaved siblings, the Amandas' and the Susans', to remove from weary shoulders their heavy cloaks of sadness and social isolation and instead replace them with comforting shawls of self-assurance and social interaction.

9

Impact of Major Life Transitions on Adolescent Development

Sandra L. Elder, M.Ed

Our youth love luxury; they have bad manners, contempt for authority, they show disrespect for elders and love chatter in place of exercise. Children are now tyrants, not the servants of their households. They no longer rise when elders enter the room. They contradict their parents, chatter before company, gobble up their food, and tyrannize their teachers. [Plato quoting Socrates in the fifth century B.C.]

The above description is very similar to what might be written about adolescents in the 1980s. Yet in psychological terms the twentieth-century adolescent matures more rapidly and in sociological terms, due to a delay in economic and social independence (a direct result of the need for post-secondary training in our highly competitive work force: Froese 1975), is staying younger for a longer period of time. Kettle (1986) lists some of the things that have happened to make this generation of adolescents different. They are the first generation of high school graduates; the only generation that was raised in an economic boom; the first generation raised with television; the first drug generation; the first urban generation; the first generation to be substantial victims of divorce, and the first generation brought up in a welfare state.

Today's adolescents are frequently overprotected, overindulged, and often overly dependent. The phenomenal advances in technology can overwhelm adolescents and immobilize them. They have lived all their lives in a rapidly changing world and can not settle for gradual changes: They have had limited experience with what it means to delay gratification. Their response to these changes is often withdrawal into a nondemanding, nonworking world, or maintaining a level of stimulation through the use of drugs, music, and sex in an attempt to combat symptoms of depression (Levine et al. 1972).

90

Coleman (1980) describes adolescence as being a complex and contradictory stage of development, encompassing many opposites and extremes. Adjustment in adolescence has critical implications for adult development. There is a preference now for viewing adolescence as a transitional process rather than a stage. This transition results from the operation of a number of pressures. Some of these pressures, the physiological and emotional, are internal, while other pressures originate from external influences, i.e., peers, parents, teachers, and society at large. It is the interplay of these forces that, in the final analysis, contributes more than anything else to the success or failure of the transition from childhood to adulthood. The great majority of adolescents cope well with the problems of adjustment inherent in the transitional process; however, there are those who are vulnerable to the stresses and strains. Identifying these "at risk" adolescents becomes the basis for the establishment of preventive, interventive, and postventive programs.

Adolescence is a transitional process when an individual's mental health is especially susceptible to both personal and environmental stresses. Some of the major developmental tasks create stresses (Erikson 1963). Freeman (1987) identifies five developmental issues that confront adolescents:

(1) identity: self-concept, body image, racial identity, and sexual identity;
(2) separation from the family of origin (in emotional, functional, and financial areas);
(3) friendship: appropriate and satisfying peer relationships;
(4) courtship: relationships with the opposite sex; and
(5) career planning and career choice.

Although each of these issues may be confronted to some degree during other developmental phases, the tasks and the intensity of focus pertain uniquely to adolescence. Developmental issues are interrelated. Adolescents work on them in combination rather than in an isolated or sequential manner. The responses to some of these issues can have either a positive or negative effect on how the issues are handled. Whether adolescents experience such developmental changes as a loss depends on several factors: the quality of the relationships between adolescents and significant others; lack of opportunity or knowledge to anticipate and plan for changes; and the adolescent's perspective about developmental changes (Freeman 1987).

Adolescence has been conceptualized as the age of transitions that bridges the gap between childhood and adulthood. Psychological upheaval and emotional turmoil are often the consequence of major psychological transitions during adolescence. It is the adolescent's experience of transitions that determines their emotional significance and impact (Healy and Stewart 1984). During times of turmoil it is helpful to rely on others who have experienced or are experiencing the same transitions.

Erikson's (1963) theory of psychosocial development contends that adolescents pass through clearly delineated stages in which specific types of conflicts are resolved. The way in which adolescents resolve these conflicts will influence their adult personalities. He views personality as developing throughout the life span with adolescence being a particularly decisive period for forming an identity. Life holds in store for us over the course of our development predictable psychosocial crises. These crises do not pose a threat of catastrophe but rather they represent turning points or "crucial periods of increased vulnerability and heightened potential." The resolution of these crises can result in a new balance of forces within the individual. Failure to negotiate these crises presents limitations to the individual's capacity for further development (Hayes 1981).

For many young people the transition from childhood to adulthood is marked by an upsurge in depressive feelings, uncertainty about the future, and an increased risk of psychological disorder. Delinquency and drug abuse, as well as depressive conditions, become much more common during adolescence. New capacities emerge and existing capacities increase. Cognitive skills as well as social and emotional skills become more developed. These changes do not happen spontaneously but have to be learned and experienced in interactions with other people. All of us have to learn, relearn, and unlearn constantly. All changes do not take place at the same time.

Coleman (1980) concludes by identifying what he refers to as being the "even needs" of adolescents in our society:

(1) adults who will exercise their authority with adolescents but still allow them to be a part of the decision making process;
(2) participation in the adult world;
(3) being viewed as individuals and not only as members of a group;
(4) opportunities to utilize and develop their own level of formal operational thought;
(5) help understanding their sexuality;
(6) opportunities to become involved in peer group activities; and
(7) help with understanding that there are stresses inherent in the transitional process.

Ingersoll and Orr (1988) discuss the fact that normal adolescence requires the completion of a variety of socially and psychologically defined developmental tasks. The impact of the transitional life events on adolescents depends on the value given them by the individual (Johnson 1986; Healy and Stewart 1984). The transition from junior to senior high school may be negative for one individual but positive for another. Significant life events may, however, have a generalized disruptive effect on an individual's ability to cope. The adolescent who experiences several major life events may be overwhelmed and unable to cope. The inability to cope with numerous life events may result in the development of negative feelings about himself. Low self-esteem can result in individuals becoming involved in self-destructive behaviors.

The onset of adolescence may be sudden, taking the child, parent, and society by surprise or it may come on gradually over weeks, months, or even years. The stresses thus set up among the adolescent, his parents, and society seem almost inevitable, since each makes a different demand on the individual. The adolescent struggles with attempts at becoming independent while parents and society expect him to experience transition smoothly. At the same time, he finds himself subjected to social pressures and group influences. It is a process that is still in some respects extremely regimented as a result of parental and societal pressures, and yet on the other hand is in some respects extremely free. It is a period when the adolescent is vulnerable to emotional stresses and strains, especially when he feels that the freedom that is extended to him is precarious, for it still has the restraints of parents and society imposed upon it (Froese 1975).

Adolescent alienation is a process in which there is a loss of, or an estrangement from, some well established relationship in the absence of a viable alternative. There is negative connotation, which implies a distancing of a previous desirable relationship. This distancing can be either a conscious or an unconscious withdrawal from parents, adults, or society itself. Or it may be a feeling on the part of the adolescent that he has been isolated and shut out by his parents, adults, and society. Whether alienation originates with the adolescent, or whether it is forced upon him, he ends up feeling isolated and the meaningful parental relationships previously so important must in some way be replaced. This is why, in adolescence more than any other time of life, emotionally close peer relationships are of crucial importance. Too many adolescents have failed to replace the earlier relationships and end up suffering from feelings of emptiness, loneliness, boredom, or unreality. Because the process of alienation gradually creates distance between the adolescent and his parents, adults, and society, how individual members of these groups respond to the adolescent is of vital importance. Cambor states that most adolescents who run into difficulty have suffered early psychic trauma that interferes with the normal progressive and synchronous unfolding of maturation and development. The adolescent may manifest a poorly defined sense of self by complaining of a lack of feelings, or of feelings of boredom, emptiness, isolation, and inadequacy. There may be an associated lack of goals and direction, characterized by the manifestation of an impaired capacity for meaningful relationship to their own internal world (Froese 1975).

Emotional turbulence versus emotional flatness during adolescence is often a direct result of the process of continuous growth and adaptation to discrete life changes. Healy and Stewart have postulated four notions to support the idea that life changes even when stressful can provide opportunities for growth and development: (1) that life changes are stressful and disequilibrating and often interrupt relatively stable emotional adaptations; (2) that life changes are diseqilibrating and stressful only if they are meaningful to the individual experiencing them and result in an increase in novel stimuli to be mastered; (3) that life changes that are meaningful and result in an increase in novel stimuli to mastery, precipitate a return to a fairly primitive emotional state toward the environment; and (4) that individuals should adopt alternative responses to their environment, i.e., autonomy, assertion and integration. Adolescents who do not recover from the disequilibration and do not attain a new emotional adaptation are often those individuals who lack the resources to facilitate their adaptation or who are faced with obstacles to normal development, i.e., parents who block the growth of independence. This may result in a preoccupation with one of the earlier reactions—or the process of emotional adaptation may occur at a much slower rate.

In order to facilitate growth, intervention is most useful at normal developmental crisis points, at which time clear issues are faced and tasks mastered if growth and maturation are to continue (Erikson 1963). Adjusting to new ways of thinking is one of the most difficult tasks confronting adolescents (Elkind 1984). Adolescents are often idealistic, critical, argumentative, self-conscious (imaginary audience), self-centered (personal fable) hypocritical, and subject to extreme emotional swings.

According to Elkind, the adolescent stage of development has been excised from the life cycle and adolescents have been given an adulthood with all of the responsibilities but few of the prerogatives. Young people today are quite literally all grown up with no place to go. The impact of this premature adulthood upon today's adolescents is twofold. First, the absence of that period impairs the formation of that all important self-definition. This sense of self is therefore one of the adolescent's most important defenses against stress. By impairing his or her ability to construct a secure personal identity, today's society leaves the adolescent more vulnerable and less competent to meet the challenges of life. The second impact of premature adulthood is stress. Adolescents today are more vulnerable to stress in their life while at the same time we expose them to new and more powerful stresses than were ever faced by previous generations of adolescents. The repercussions of these stressors have been the ever-increasing presence of substance abuse, pregnancy, suicides, crime, prostitution, pornography, and run-away youth.

The young people of today are exposed to numerous transitions in their daily lives. Every transition involves an ending, followed by a period of confusion and distress and finally by a new beginning. Old habits must be altered, familiar surroundings given up, and friends left behind, creating feelings of disruption and loneliness (Bridges 1982). The death of a parent, in contrast to normal developmental crises involves a separation and individuation that is complete, final, irreversible, and frequently sudden and unanticipated. Lacking experience with death as a reality and being sheltered from such an experience by parental expectations that are often vague, hasty, or evasive, the child must often deal with this loss in isolation (Murphy 1986–87). Adolescents are vulnerable and are influenced by society's attitudes about death and loss. The fact that we have created a world that tends to support the denial of death in our lives creates additional barriers to any healthy resolution (Kastenbaum). Programs that directly address these issues will pave the way for providing the necessary information that adolescents need to establish a healthy completion of developmental tasks. These programs will also help grieving adolescents to relabel their reactions to these experiences and influence the quality of their lives (Ewalt and Perkins 1979).

Intervention at naturally occurring crisis points in an adolescent's life is often most useful in helping them through this transitional process in a way that facilitates growth while preventing the development of maladaptive solutions. The introduction of time-limited groups is described as a means of helping "normal" adolescents understand and cope with this stage of development. These groups are designed to offer adolescents the opportunity to face, discuss, and sometimes resolve their fears, concerns, and anxieties about significant life transitions. The Objectives are based on Worden's four tasks of mourning: (1) to accept the reality of the loss; (2) to experience the pain of grief; (3) to adjust to an environment in which the significant person no longer exists; and (4) to withdraw emotional energy and to reinvest it in other relationships. After an individual sustains loss, these tasks of mourning must be accomplished for equilibrium to be reestablished and the grief process to be completed.

The goals of these programs are: (1) to create an atmosphere for sharing information, ideas, and feelings regarding death and loss issues; (2) to develop an understanding and awareness of normal grief reactions; (3) to gain a better understanding and appreciation of death and loss in order to develop a better quality of life; (4) to create the opportunity for giving and receiving support to and from one another; and (5) to identify and enhance specific coping skills and tasks that will help to deal with death and loss issues. The format is based on both a preventive and interventive model or relabeling of adolescents' reactions to death and loss. The relabeling process will help adolescents to see that they cannot change the circumstances in their lives but they can change their responses to them.

Working with "normal" adolescents who are faced with significant life transitions is both a challenge and a most rewarding experience for the individuals who serve as group leaders, trainers, and consultants. Weinberger and Reuter (1980) describe this experience as being an opportunity to learn about adolescence and the concept of "normality." They feel that working with a clinic-referred population gives the clinician a distorted view of adolescence: These groups enhance the clinician's awareness of the adolescent's capacity to cope with significant life transitions. The groups can reaffirm belief in the adolescent's lack of fragility and their underlying strength. It also provides the arena for broadening one's own definitions of what is "health" and what is "pathology".

References

Bridges, W. 1982. *Transitions: Making sense of life's changes.* Menlo Park, CA: Addison-Westley.

Cambor, G. 1973. Adolescent alienation syndrome. In J. C. Schoolar, ed. *Current Issues in Adolescent Psychiatry.* New York: Brunner-Mazel.

Coleman, J. 1980. *The nature of adolescence.* London, England: Methuen.

Elkind, D. 1984. *All grown up and no place to go: Teenagers in crisis.* Menlo Park, CA: Addison-Westley.

Erikson, E. 1963. *Childhood and society.* 2nd ed. New York: W.W. Norton.

Ewalt, P. and L. Perkins. 1979. The real experience of death among adolescents. *Journal of Contempary Social Work* 60:547–51.

Freeman, E. 1987. Interaction of pregnancy, loss and developmental issues in adolescents. *Journal of Contempary Social Work* 68(1):38–46.

Froese, A. 1975. Adolescence. *Canada's Mental Health* 23(1):9–12.

Hayes, R. 1981. High School Graduation: The case for identity loss. *The Personnal and Guidance Journal* 59 (February):369–71.

Healy, J. and A. Stewart. 1984. Adaptation to life changes in adolescence. P. Karoly J. Steffen, eds. *Adolescent behavior disorders: Foundations and Contempary Concerns.* Vol. 3. Lexington, KY: D.C. Heath.

Ingersoll, G. and D. Orr. 1988. Adolescents at risk. *Counseling and Human Development* 20 (6):1–8.

Johnson, J.H. 1986. Life events as stressors in childhood and adolescence. *Developmental Clinical Psychology* 8.

Kettle, J. 1986. Some thoughts on the big generation growing up. *Journal of Child Care* Summer: 9–17.

Lamers, W. 1981. How doctors feel when a patient dies [Grief is the price for love]. In E. Grollman, ed. *What helped me when my loved one died.* Boston: Beacon Press.

Levine, S., D. Lloyd and W. Longdon. 1972. The speed user: Social and psychological factors in amphetamie abuse. *Canadian Psychiatirc Association Journal* 17:229–41.

Murphy, P.A. 1986–87. Parental death in childhood and loneliness in young adults. *Omega* 17 (3):219–28.

Weinberger, G. and M. Reuter. 1980. The "life discussion" group as a means of facilitating personal growth and development in late adolescence. *Journal of Clinical Child Psychology* 9 (1):6–12.

Werner, E. and R. Smith. 1982. *Vulnerable but not invincible: A longitudunal study of resilient children and youth.* New York: McGraw-Hill.

Worden, W. 1982. *Grief counselling and grief therapy.* New York: Springer Publishing.

10

The Funeral Director and the Grieving Child

Duane Weeks, MA

In the early winter of 1984, I was called to Los Angeles to help with the funeral arrangements for my cousin's husband. Leonard was survived by his wife, three children, and several grandchildren. During one visit to the funeral home, I picked up Leonard's three-year-old grandson, carried him over to the casket, and answered some of his questions. His first question was "Where are his legs?" On the West Coast, most of the caskets we use are only opened halfway, so the body is only shown from the hips up, with the legs covered. I put the boy down, opened the bottom half of the casket, and lifted him again so he could see his grandfather's legs. Question one answered. His second question was "Can I touch him?" The answer, of course, was yes, and he did touch him, which led to the third question, "Why is he so cold?" This is a little trickier question for a three year old, but I explained how we are warm because our body is working and the blood is running through us, but when we die, our body and the blood stop working. When our body stops working, we get just as warm or cold as the room we are in, and that is why his grandpa's body felt so cold. By this time he had endured enough explanation, so he squirmed down and went to stand beside his mother, who thanked me and said, "You know, I have often wondered myself why bodies in caskets feel so cold. Thanks for explaining it to us." This, I think, is one of the important lessons about talking with children. Like the children's sermon in church, adults often pay as much attention, respond as well, and get as much from the discussion for children as do the children. Working with the children can be equally important for the children and the adults.

Eighty years ago children would have picked up on much of this death education naturally. They lived in larger extended families, life expectancies were short, and death was a natural part of their lives. Now, however, children live in smaller nuclear families, we have long life expectancies, and death, which occurs mostly in hospitals, nursing homes, or other institutions, appears unnatural. This means that those of us in the caregiving professions must be more sensitive to the needs of the children, as well as providing for the needs of the surviving adults.

What appears to be happening in western society is that many adults are feeling unable to deal with the physical and emotional trauma generated by dying and death, and are turning to caregivers to provide care for the dying and dead, as well as the grieving and mourning. These caregivers—physicians, teachers, nurses, funeral directors, psychologists, social workers—are expected and needed to assist both the dying and the surviving with the process of grief. This delegation of responsibility is not, of course, limited to death-related issues. We hand our little children over to preschools where surrogate parents may or may not give them love and attention until they are old enough to be enrolled in a regular school class. When they are enrolled in regular school, we send them, after school, to play at a daycare center until we take them home for a microwaved supper in front of the television set, where delegated performers entertain us until we go to bed. We exist this way month after month, until vacation time comes and we enjoy a trip to foreign lands while our children enjoy another "learning experience" at summer camp. This scenario continues until we begin to slow down and our children, who really don't know us anyway, use our money to place us under the care of other professionals: physicians in hospitals, nurses in nursing homes, and undertakers in funeral homes.

These caregivers, to whom has been delegated the responsibility of accommodating the dying and facilitating the grieving, are ill prepared for this responsibility. Research done in 1986 indicates that less than 42 percent of the funeral directors, 36 percent of the physicians, and less than 2 percent of the teachers have had any death education to prepare them for working with the dying and grieving. Of those who had death education, 62 percent of the funeral directors, 70 percent of the physicians, and 100 percent of the teachers responded that their death education was not adequate to meet their needs. Although none of these three categories contain practitioners who generally feel well prepared to deal with death issues, funeral directors are apparently better prepared than those in the other two occupations, at least as far as their death education is concerned (Weeks 1986). This research uncovered teachers frustrated at their inability to deal with children who are grieving—particularly apparent since the *Challenger* disaster occurred only four months before the research was done.

In addition to being more knowledgable about death, funeral directors are shown to be more helpful to the survivors. Research begun by Phyllis Silverman (1986) characterizes funeral directors as the most helpful, the most professionally supportive, most sensitive and understanding, and most highly accepted of all helping professionals by surviving families. The situation is not, unfortunately, that funeral directors are doing so much so well that nothing is required of the other professions. Rather, the situation appears to be that everyone is doing very little, with the funeral directors performing just a little better than those in the other professions.

If adults who are grieving are unable to find or get the help they need, then we must understand that children, who are unlikely to understand what they need or how to find help, are still less likely to find answers and solutions.

One problem—and solution—is communication. If we can communicate with children, learning what they are feeling and being comfortable with them in discussing those feelings, we can be very helpful to their working through the grief process.

Communication between an adult and a small child can be difficult because small children are often afraid of adults and threatened by our size; often we adults cannot understand what the small child means. Communication between an adult and an adolescent is also difficult. Adults are often threatened by the maturation of adolescents, a process that seems to encourage independence, hostility, and mistrust, three factors that are detrimental to the healing of grief.

In order to facilitate open communication, I will often let the child know how I feel about this, or a similar, situation. If, for example, a child's father has died, I will tell her how I felt when my father died. This sharing of feelings increases the child's trust in me. When I am willing to express my thoughts and feelings openly in front of that child, she understands that I trust her and have confidence in her. Thus, she understands that she can trust me and have confidence in me. She will not hurt me and I will not hurt her. We establish a mutual trust and rapport.

It is important that the child not perceive an adult as talking down to her. Usually the child and I, sometimes with other adults, will be sitting around a small round conference table. We will talk about lots of things like puppies and pretty dresses and favorite toys. We just talk and get to know one another, eyeball to eyeball. If we are with the body, I will try to get well enough acquainted with the child so I can hold her up to look into the casket; we touch things and ask and answer questions. Sometimes we sit together on the floor, even with other adults, and look at the flowers or talk about things. It is important to discuss these "things" because it allows a child with a short span of attention to mentally wander in and out of the death focus, and yet still feel comfortable around death and the body. It is sometimes easier to talk with children without other members of the child's family present. Those family members may be uncomfortable with some of a child's questions, some of the answers, or may simply be overly protective of the child.

The cemetery is a great place for discussing death with little children. They love to look at the different grave stones, jump over the smaller, flat markers, and peer down into the depth of the grave. Last year two preschool girls, their mother and I went to the cemetery about a month after their little brother was buried. We read his grave marker and talked about where he was and whether or not he could hear us talking. We ran around the cemetery and lay on our backs watching the clouds float overhead as we talked and remembered their brother.

Three years ago I was at King's College listening to Sandra Bertman discuss art and death, when I realized I was ignoring a very important aspect of communication with children: their drawings. Since that time I have found it helpful to have children draw what they feel about death. If a child draws the picture and then explains it to me, we have a really good basis for discussion. I have discovered that a small box of crayons is an excellent communication investment. Robin, age four, and Georgia, five and one-half, were asked to draw two pictures of their baby brother. The first was a picture of him while he was alive. The second was a picture of him after he died. Robin drew a happy, smiling brother for her first picture; in the second, her brother was not shown, only his grave with flowers around it. Georgia's first picture showed her smiling brother in his bassinet. The sun could be seen shining brightly through the window. In Georgia's second picture she drew her brother in a hospital (he was found dead in his crib at home), using purple to symbolize death as he lay in his casket, and she drew herself beside the casket.

There is not enough research to conclude that children at any age react in a specific manner toward death. However, there is evidence that allows us to generalize about their reactions at different age levels. Richard Lonetto (1980) presents studies that suggest different concepts of death at different age levels. The research that is presented by Lonetto is representative of other research done on attitudes of children toward death.

The first confrontations with death occur for a child between the ages of three and five. Children of this age view death as reversible and temporary, as living on with changes. Lonetto suggests that children between six and eight begin to see death as more personal, brought on by some external object like the death-man, skeletons, or ghosts and as something that can be avoided. Nine to twelve year olds conceptualize death as universal, unavoidable, and final: "They manifest a maturity of concepts similar to those held by adults."

In spite of the plethora of studies on children and death, there are those who say that children are innocent, never thinking about death. These folks should consider television, where on any given Saturday morning any child old enough to turn on the television can see and be confused by temporary death. Temporary death is portrayed by cartoons like the (beep beep) Roadrunner cartoons, where

Wiley Coyote chases the Roadrunner but is crushed dead by a rock, only to return in the following cartoon segment where he chases the Roadrunner, and runs off the edge of a gigantic cliff, returning yet again to chase the Roadrunner until he is blown up by dynamite, only to return. . . . Temporary, confusing death is also portrayed in the old Westerns and dramas, where the bad guy is killed and everything is fine, until the next time that same bad guy is shown in another movie, very much alive.

The medium of television has also allowed us to bring real deaths into our homes. Television has portrayed the tragedies of war in Vietnam and El Salvador, catastrophic earthquakes in Columbia and Mexico, and the deaths of our neighbors from homicides, auto accidents, and airplane disasters. Our children, like no previous generation, live in the shadow of nuclear death. They see television coverage of antinuclear demonstrations and they hear about nuclear build ups. For months, the name Chernobyl was mentioned regularly on newscasts and brought mental images of nuclear devastation. Television makes death seem temporary, and it makes death appear to be something that happens to others, not us. After the January 1986, *Challenger* tragedy, which deeply hurt and confused many children, one little girl came up to her teacher and said, "They will be O.K., that just happened on television."

Whatever the child's age, there is no place for dishonesty or fairy tale explanations. In the misguided attempts to protect children, adults sometimes say things that cause harmful responses. When we attempt to protect children, we are really only protecting ourselves from temporarily uncomfortable feelings that we are attempting to avoid and that the questions may address. For example, if we answer a question about the death of a child's grandfather by replying that grandfather went on a long trip, the child may have questions, some of which he may be afraid to express verbally, such as: "Why didn't grandpa say good-by?" or "Will he bring me a present when he comes back?" or "Is today the day grandpa gets back?" After a while, serious questions can become devastating. A young woman tells of the death of her father when she was three. For seven years her mother told her that her father was away on business. "I wondered every day until I was ten," she related, "what a little girl could have done to make her daddy so mad he would leave her without even kissing her good-by."

It is important to tell all children plainly what is happening. Funeral directors do not wish to usurp the authority of a family member, clergy, or friend, but we should have no difficulty in telling a child:

1. This is a very (very, very, very) sad time.
2. What "dead" means.

3. They did not cause the death. (Children often confuse illegitimate grief with legitimate grief, believing they caused the death.)
4. What is happening, what will happen.
5. Whatever they feel (including relief) is okay.
6. Choices are theirs.
7. How I (others) feel.

Older children may have had some experience of death; the death of a goldfish, other pets, or a distant relative. Not only are these experiences helpful in preparing a child for grieving when the death of a significant other occurs, they are useful to recall to the child's mind when that significant death does occur.

Very often when a family is planning a funeral service, the question arises as to whether or not children should view the body or attend the funeral services. The answers are unclear, with much depending on what the child wishes to do and to what extent she would like to be involved in the final rituals. When a child, whether a small child or a teenager, comes to the funeral home prior to the funeral service, we try to take him on a brief tour of the facility, showing him the chapel, where he will be sitting, where the rest rooms are, and explaining what will happen during the service. If he has any questions we answer them. This brief introduction to the funeral home makes the building seem familiar and less formidable when the child comes to the service.

Dan Schaefer, author of *How Do We Tell The Children?* (1986), suggests that how you ask a child whether or not he wants to attend funeral services will obtain predictably different responses. You can ask, "You don't want to go to the funeral, do you?" or "You want to go to the funeral, don't you?" or "Would you like to go to the funeral?" Grollman (1967), believes that children should attend the funeral and states that: "A youngster should have the same right as any other member of the family to attend the funeral and to offer his last respects and to express his own love and devotion." However McCown (1984) finds more behavior problems among children who attended funerals for their siblings than among those who did not. There is not a unanimous consensus on whether or not children should attend funerals.

Viewing of the body may be helpful to children, provided there are not present "helpful" adults who insist on forcing the child to "kiss Uncle Bill" or who try to "protect" the child by keeping her away from the casket and body. There does not seem to be any empirical evidence on whether or not viewing of the body is helpful for people of any age, let alone children. It seems, however, that viewing of the body would promote questions from a child that should be answered correctly and with sensitivity. Viewing a body could underscore the reality of death for a child; it might ease the thoughts that have been created by the child's vivid imagination.

When funeral arrangements are made and the extended family includes pre-teenage children, grandchildren, or close nephews or nieces, an adult close to that child, preferably a parent, is given a copy of Grollman's *Talking About Death* (1970). This is a dialogue between parent and child, intended to help explain the concept of death. Parents are encouraged to read the introduction and parents guide before using the dialogue with their child. If a child is old enough to read comfortably and does not want to be held and read to, she can read this book herself and gain much useful information.

When I am talking to children old enough to read, I suggest that they might really enjoy reading chapter eight of *Bambi* (Salten 1928). Chapter eight is the poignant dialogue between two autumn leaves, concerning life and death. This dialogue, recently revised and popularized as *The Fall of Freddie the Leaf* (Buscaglia 1982), is an excellent illustration of nature's life cycle. Older children, who are accomplished readers, are often loaned copies of books from our funeral home library. *I Heard the Owl Call My Name* (Craven 1973), *On Death and Dying* (Kubler-Ross 1969), *A Grief Observed* (Lewis 1963), *Eric* (Lund 1974), *The Courage to Grieve* (Tatelbaum 1980), and *A Severe Mercy* (Vanauken 1977), are excellent books for teen or young adult readers.

Fourteen years ago I approached Catherine Johnson, a psychology instructor at Enumclaw High School, about introducing a death unit into the psychology curriculum. She thought the idea was good, and so we developed a death education unit for high school seniors. This unit is offered for three weeks each semester and the students indicate that it is one of the highlights of their high school studies. Not only does this give me an excellent opportunity to address the death issues with those psychology students, but it gives them some basic information and understanding so that they can be good Samaritans, helpful to their friends and family when a death occurs.

Teenage children can be difficult to understand; their need for independence and "macho" attitude may make them difficult to approach as well. Ms. Johnson, the psychology instructor, has also formed an active grief support group for students at Enumclaw High School. Those students who are grieving the death of someone close to them may attend these open-ended meetings where students share their feelings, frustrations, and expectations with one another. Conversations are confidential and that confidentiality is highly respected. There are times when I will suggest to students that they investigate or join that support group; other times I will be asked to talk with different students in the group.

In addition to that support group, we are fortunate to have in our local area a physician, an attorney, four counselors, one teacher, and two ministers to whom I can comfortably refer children who seem to need special grief counseling. In our small town, we do not compete for the attention of those who need our help. It is not funeral directors against the clergy or hospice workers against the teachers or anyone against anyone else. We cooperate and communicate. We believe that it is all of us, working together, who will help the children as they try to understand and accept the reality and finality of death.

For the past 25 years, funeral directors have been the forgotten element in death education and counseling. A quick perusal of the psychology, sociology, or medical abstracts shows that articles about physicians and death, teachers and death, nurses and death, social workers and death, clergy and death abound. Outside of the funeral trade journals it is difficult to find any articles or research dealing with funeral directors and death.

It is important for everyone involved with the shaping of young lives to realize that the funeral director should be an important means of support when grief affects these young people. It is the funeral director who is often the major influence—outside of the immediate family—on the young person. It is also the funeral director whom the family sees most often during the period of intense grief between the death and the funeral. It is the funeral director, using experience, knowledge, and intuition, who often realizes that a young person is responding to death in a seemingly inappropriate manner. And sometimes it is the funeral director, representative of a steady, outside influence, to whom the young person turns.

Here are some methods that we have found helpful in working with teenagers who have experienced the death of someone close to them.

— We don't believe the mask, the front, the indifference that says "Everything is fine." That is often a mask the teen herself wants removed.
— We encourage the children or grandchildren to participate in the funeral service planning and, if they like, to participate in the funeral ritual. Almost always the residing minister, priest, rabbi, or other officiant is pleased to include them.
— We let the teens know that their ideas and input for funeral arrangements are important and valid, and will be listened to.
— We encourage open talking and crying, and we legitimize anger.
— We encourage hugging, if the child is comfortable with the contact.
— We ask the teenagers, privately if possible, if they want time alone to view the body or just spend some time in the room with the body.
— We remind them that we are always available—and we are—to answer questions and talk with them not only at the time of the death but whenever they might want to afterward. For example, a high school student once called me about 3:00 A.M. He was at a party, drunk, and pretty profane. We talked for a few minutes until he began talking about the death of his mother and what a difficult time he was having. After several more minutes he became thoughtful and apologetic, and

I invited him to come in during the day to visit me. The next week he did come in, apologized again for bothering me during the night, and thanked me for helping him put some thoughts about his mother in perspective.

— We offer, again privately if possible, to be an intermediary with the other family members to express the teen's needs. Too often they just do not want to be an additional burden to their parents or other family members at an already emotional time.

— We try to reassure the children that their needs are legitimate and they need to tune into themselves so that they and other people can know what will make them feel better.

— We encourage children, especially teenagers, to keep a log of questions and concerns that they have. If they do not get suitable responses from their families, or if they are more comfortable talking to us, then we give them answers or help them seek the answers. We are always willing to call a physician to interpret clearly the cause of death or call an attorney to resolve a legal concern.

— When a student suffers the death of some significant person, we notify school personnel so that administration, teachers, and counselors can be aware of increased stress in that student's life. For example, one high school senior whose parents were killed in an automobile crash during the fall of his junior year said that he had no recollection of anything that happened during that year, even though he attended classes and earned straight A's. Another high school student, who was not allowed by her teacher to attend the grief support group, said that it took all of her concentration, all of her effort during class to keep from crying. We believe notification of school personnel can greatly improve the student's reintegration into the school society.

A Bill of Rights for Grieving Children

Bills of Rights have been developed for children caught in their parents' divorce, for children who feel guilty when saying no, and for students. Here is a Bill of Rights for children who are grieving because of a death:

1. You have the right to your own feelings. Your feelings are neither right or wrong, they are just feelings.
2. You have the right to express your grief and be comforted. If you do not get comfort, you have the right to request additional support.
3. You have the right to continued loving care, but you must understand that it may sometimes be difficult for those who love you to provide that care.

4. You have the right to help plan and to participate in the funeral rites, as much or as little as you wish.
5. You have the right to ask any questions and receive thoughtful, honest answers.
6. You have the right to be treated as an interested and important individual, not as someone's "kid."
7. If you are a surviving sibling, you have the right to maintain your own identity, without any transference of any kind from your dead sibling.
8. You have the right to grieve for days and years, however long it takes you to feel good again. There is no set time to feel better.
9. You have the right to be free from guilt, or continued grief, and you have the right to counseling if you need or want it.
10. You have the right to be a comforter to others who are grieving, to share your grief and their grief, making you both feel better.

References

Buscaglia, L. 1982. *The fall of Freddy the leaf.* New York: Holt, Rinehart, and Winston.

Craven, M. 1973. *I heard the owl call my name.* New York: Dell Publishing.

Grollman, E. 1967. *Explaining death to children.* Boston: Beacon Press.

———1970. *Talking about death.* Boston: Beacon Press.

Kubler-Ross, E. 1969. *On death and dying.* New York: Macmillan.

Lewis, C.S. 1963. *A grief observed.* New York: Seabury.

Lonetto, R. 1980. *Children's conceptions of death.* New York: Springer Publishing.

Lund, D. 1974. *Eric.* New York: Dell Publishing.

McCown, D. 1984. Funeral attendance, cremation, and young siblings. *Death Education* 8:349–63.

Salten, F. 1928. *Bambi.* Garden City: Simon and Schuster.

Schaefer, D. 1986. *How do we tell the children?* New York: Newmarket Press.

Silverman, P. 1986. *Widow to widow.* New York: Springer Publishing.

Tatelbaum, J. 1980. *The courage to grieve.* New York: Harper and Row.

Vanauken, S. 1977. *A severe mercy.* New York: Harper and Row.

Weeks, D. 1986. *Death Education for Aspiring Physicians, Teachers, and Funeral Directors.* Ann Arbor, MI: University Microfilms.

Part III

The Role of the School
in Dealing with Bereaved Teenagers

11

Guidelines for Dealing with Traumatic Events in the School Community

Sharon L. Cobb, MA

As a health educator for the Ypsilanti Public Schools for the past nineteen years, I have had ample opportunity to observe tragedies and their affect on the students and staff of a school. Fourteen years of teaching the Loss and Grief unit of a full-year Health Course, made it obvious that individual losses were dealt with haphazardly, if at all.

While a group of facilitator for a support group in the Substance Abuse program, it became apparent to me that many of the students became involved with substances due to a loss—death, separation, divorce. They had observed adults easing their pain with alcohol, so they used it too. Some of the substance abuse groups have since become groups for dealing with loss and grief issues. At the time these issues were being discussed in the groups there was a drastic increase in the number of tragedies affecting young people in surrounding districts. Except for two deaths to cancer during one summer, we had not been affected by the death of a student in eight years. With what was happening around us and what was evident from individual tragedies, we felt sure we needed a plan of action for dealing with a tragedy that might affect many individuals and possibly disrupt the educational community.

The *Guidelines* Program

Guidelines was prepared by two high school staff members, Ed Swartz and myself, in response to events that were occurring in neighboring area schools, and after we experienced our own tragedy. *Guidelines* was reviewed by eight interested staff persons and administrators. The professionals involved perceived a need for a set of procedures to eliminate contagion and deal with the impact of such events immediately, in hope of alleviating long-term effects and allowing people to return to the business at hand as quickly as possible. Clearly, more needs to be done than a moment of silence.

Responsibilities

Responsibilities for implementation are divided between the Administration Team and the Crisis Team. A major element of the procedures that promotes their effectiveness is the role of the Building Team. This team is composed of interested staff with knowledge of grief reactions and the grieving process. Staff members familiar with the affected students augment the Crisis Team.

Implementation

These procedures provide both immediate and long-term steps to be followed in times of crisis to control contagion and assist students overwhelmed by the situation. These steps eliminate guesswork and prevent the omission of important considerations. They provide consistency and allow flexibility in dealing with traumatic events. The rights and obligations of survivors are outlined and defined. Steps for implementation of the *Guidelines* provide procedures for:

1) Notification Responsibilities
2) Contact with Media
3) Staff Notification and Phone Fan Out
4) Information Dissemination—P.A. Announcement
5) Information Dissemination—Staff Memorandum
6) Maintain Normalcy
7) Crisis Rooms
8) Student Support
9) Follow-Up

These implementation procedures assure that all information released is consistent and factual; they perform a "rumor control" function while protecting the privacy of the individual. Survivorship levels and their significance, follow-up activities ranging from funeral home support to long-term grief support groups, and means for evaluating student recovery/readiness for closure are defined within the plan.

The Guidelines Themselves

The following are the Guidelines as they were approved by the Ypsilanti Board of Education in January 1987. Prior to their receiving Board approval and becoming an official district-wide procedure, they had been implemented four times and shown themselves to be a workable procedure valuable in maintaining the educational process.

Guidelines for Dealing with Death or Traumatic Events in the School Community

RATIONALE

Because tragedies occur that affect the students and staff of a school, this plan of action and the Crisis Team have been developed to provide a methodology for meeting a crisis and providing the optimum support for those involved, with minimal disruption of the educational process.

It is implicit in this plan that each person grieves in their own way, and latitude and support must be provided. This plan, based on a "worst case" scenario, can be adapted by degrees to include any situation involving death or traumatic experience in the life of a student or staff person.

This plan will address the following rights and obligations of survivors:

Rights of Survivors

1. Right to be acknowledged as a survivor.
2. Right to be informed of the facts and subsequent actions taken.
3. Right to be allowed to participate in traditional or creative leave-taking ceremonies.

Obligations of a Survivor Group

1. To acknowledge publicly the group's survivorship status.
2. To make a tangible response to defined immediate survivors on behalf of the group.
3. To make a tangible response within the group which will benefit group members.

GOAL STATEMENTS

1. To provide support to those of the educational community when one of ours is lost.
2. To acknowledge the death and affirm the life of the survivors.
3. To provide an organized, systematic, but flexible approach to dealing with tragedy.
4. To demonstrate that the grieving process is a natural part of the chain of events following any loss.
5. To reflect on the significance of that member to the school.

6. To allow the school to make a tangible response to defined immediate survivors on behalf of the school.
7. To bring consolation and comfort to the group(s).
8. To provide follow-up resources for survivors, as needed.

RESPONSIBILITIES

Administration

1. Designate one administrator for ALL media contact.
2. Schedule and chair staff meeting.
3. Appoint an administrator and designee for hall/crowd control.
4. Arrange for classroom coverage and Team members needing substitutes.
5. Assist in developing guidelines for memorials.
6. Approve student check-out.
7. Make appropriate P.A. announcement and follow-up memo for staff.
8. Coordinate staff and funeral attendance.
9. Appoint Team Leader and alternate.
10. Seek consultation from others in district.
11. Prepare notes to be sent home to parents regarding incident.
12. Notify administrators in other buildings that might be affected.

Crisis Team

1. Team Leader will coordinate team responsibilities and work directly with administration and community resource persons.
2. Make phone calls to Team and community resource persons *
3. Prepare material for staff meeting.*
4. Staff rooms to deal with crisis.
5. Facilitate support groups.
6. Assign room or rooms to be used for crisis intervention/support.
7. Work with an administrator on collecting facts and preparing press releases.*
8. One Team member will insure that each staff member has a copy of the memo and will circulate around the building to respond to inquiries from the staff.*
9. Contact family for funeral/memorial service and determine if there are other assistances the school can provide.*
10. In case of a death on the staff, a Team member will take over for

that staff member's classes, utilizing a substitute for their own classes.

11. Monitor the pay phones.

*Team Leader would probably be the best person assigned these tasks.

IMPLEMENTATION

Notification

Any person who learns of the death/traumatic event that may affect the school community should report such knowledge to the principal. The principal will then contact the Group Survivorship Team.

The Team Leader will notify the rest of the Team by phone, and Team Leader and administrator will meet immediately to decide when to begin the plan.

Options depend upon time of day that Administration/Team learn about the death/traumatic event. Plan would begin (a) start of day, (b) midday, or (c) end of day. In the case of (c), parts of plan would be instituted at the end of the day, with continuation the next morning. It is recommended that school NOT be closed, but the next day's activities altered, as needed.

The administrator and Group Survivorship Team Leader will also decide on necessary detail such as: who will lead staff meeting, who will call Community Mental Health staff member, etc. See the section on Responsibilities, which outlines the specific tasks.

In the event that buses pass the scene of an accident or death, particularly if students/staff are involved, transportation will contact the appropriate administrators. An administrator would then siphon students from those buses into an appropriate area until facts are known.

Contact with Media

Administration will designate one person to be the spokesperson for all media contact, and this should be the only staff person to talk to media. All others will refer media to this person. The media will be directed to designated area where the appointed administrator will meet with them. Administration will prepare a press release containing as many facts as possible without violating privacy laws and without containing conjecture or hearsay. A copy of this press release will be provided to the switchboard operator/building secretary. Any other non-school persons or non-media persons will be sent to designated area.

General Staff Meeting

(Steps 4 and 5 may precede a general staff meeting in the case of a morning or midday event.)

The meeting will be held as soon after notification of the event as possible. For example, if the event occurs in the morning, this voluntary meeting will be held during teacher lunch hours with a follow-up meeting after school. If the event occurs in the afternoon, meeting will be held after school. If the event occurs after school, meeting will be held first thing the next morning.

Staff will be notified of this voluntary meeting through existing phone fan out.

AGENDA

1. Administrator will give facts as known and introduce Team spokesperson.
2. Team spokesperson will outline activities for the day following this plan.
3. Team spokesperson will introduce Community Mental Health staff members (CMH).
4. CMH staff will discuss bereavement process and answer questions.
5. A handout will be distributed which lists an outline of the bereavement process, sample lesson plans, and types of behavior/reactions to be prepared for.
6. Following the presentation and Q & A session with CMH, staff will be encouraged to stay and break into small groups. These small groups would provide an opportunity for staff to deal with their own feelings of loss and grief, as well as old unresolved grief reactions which may be brought up by the current situation.
7. Team members will act as facilitators for these small group discussions, along with the CMH representatives.
8. The memo announcing the death/traumatic event will be distributed to staff for use in discussing the situation with students at the beginning of school, if not previously handed out after a P.A. announcement.

P.A. Announcement Is made

Prior to an announcement, a staff member will coordinate crowd control and be responsible for clearing the halls of students and others. All students will be under the supervision of a teacher.

A P.A. announcement will be made by an administrator announcing the death/traumatic event. This announcement should contain as many substantiated facts as possible without violating privacy laws. Avoid conjecture and hearsay, avoid gory details, avoid excess emotion—DO express feelings of loss. If not previously distributed (at general staff meeting), copies of the announcement will be distributed at this time to all classrooms. The written announcement may contain some more details then the verbal announcement, but should follow the above guidelines.

Discussion

After the P.A. announcement, teachers will read or paraphrase the written announcement. Time should be provided for questions and discussion where needed. However, returning to the regular routine as quickly as possible will be helpful.

Subsequent Classes/Activities

Throughout the balance of the day, teachers are encouraged to conduct classes and alter the content area, as necessary, to be sensitive to issues on the students' minds. Examples will be provided to the teachers at staff meeting of the kinds of activities that might be appropriate.

Crisis Rooms

Throughout the day of the crisis, students who are particularly upset will be given the option of leaving class and going to an identified crisis room. These room(s) will be staffed by one or more of the following: district social workers, Team members, school counselors, school nurse, community mental health worker, community pastoral team, etc. There should be one staff person for every 6–8 students.

Discussion might include: the story or the death/event (listen for guilt); the life of the deceased, including discussing memories; expectations regarding funeral/future, and responses of what they can do. (A good ritual is one that is widely shared by survivors.)

Group activities include: talking and sharing, comforting and calming, and writing out feelings for those who cannot express them verbally.

Students must have passes from classes to the crisis rooms. Students will return to their sending teacher five (5) minutes before the end of the hour with a pass. Students may return to the crisis room after checking with the next hour's teacher and receiving a pass. For those students who should remain in the crisis room, a note will be sent to the sending teacher by a Team member.

Check Out

Students who are particularly upset and need to leave school will be discharged to PARENTS ONLY. They are not to just leave by themselves. To leave, students must check out through standard procedure. The school nurse will evaluate any degree of physical illness that is presented, and keep track of students who leave, for whatever reason.

Follow-up

A. Team, administration, and staff should identify possible persons requiring long-term support group participation, in or out of school. The following group identifications may be useful in group formation:

Primary Survivors: Those having had a present or past significant relationships with the deceased/event, i.e., family members, intimate friends, and anyone who has had a major life interaction with the deceased/event. Also includes anyone who may have witnessed the death/traumatic event or the events leading up to it.

Secondary Survivors: Those who have had an intermediate life interaction with the deceased/event, i.e., work, classmates, friends, social acquaintances, eye witnesses, etc.

Others: Those who have had little or no interaction with the deceased/event but who share meaningful identification and experiences with the group: classmates, fellow sophomore, team member, band member, neighbor, etc.

B. Team will follow up on each student who has checked out, encouraging him/her to join a support group at school or through a community agency.

C. Develop a memorial activity with students which may include:

1. Mini-funeral or memorial service at school, followed by refreshments and a time for people to share
2. Scholarship
3. Donation to organization or group to which individual belonged
4. Plant shrubs or tree
5. Buy something for the school in the person's name
6. Wear badges or armbands
7. Group identified memoriam in the newspaper
8. Card/flowers in respect to next of kin from each group
9. Group representation at the funeral: time allowed after the funeral for those students who attended to talk about their feelings.

Clinical Applications

Since June 1986, these *Guidelines* have been implemented fourteen (14) times. Each event has been different from every other. Some of the causes may have been the same, but there the similarities have ended.

1. The first time implementation was needed there was an auto accident the last day of final exams in June as students were headed to school. Four students in two cars were involved with a third car driven by a teacher in a neighboring district. One of the victims, a very popular young man, was removed from the respirator the next morning. The Team had been called together the day before

and immediately went into action. It was teachers record day and an invitation was extended to all staff who wished to talk to meet in the conference room. A schedule was set up to cover the funeral home during visitation hours, at the funeral, and a get-together of students after the funeral before the summer vacation began. We helped 1000, 600, and 125 students respectively, and in the fall had a support group for twelve of his best friends.

2. That summer one of our students died from a heart transplant rejection. We were at the funeral home and funeral to help students.

3. In the fall of 1986, some elementary school students observed a murder while waiting for a school bus. The police notified the school and the Building Team greeted the students as they came off the bus, and took them to an area to allow them to talk and begin to work through their feelings.

4-6. We have dealt with two support staff suicides and assisted a neighboring district to deal with the suicide of one of their students. Community mental health workers had told them of our procedures and they called us. Since that time they have developed their own guidelines following ours. For our support staff suicides, their co-workers met with community mental health workers and then referrals were made for those who needed it to the Employee Assistance Program personnel.

7. There was a skateboard accident that affected a junior high (victim) and the high school (driver and brother of victim). The individual was not killed, but it was touch and go. The entire Team was not called in, but the Team Leader assisted both young men in dealing with the situation and repercussions.

8. An ex-student was murdered at 2 A.M. on a Monday morning; the Team was brought out because many of his siblings, other relatives, and friends did not find out until they reached the bus in the morning. Students were taken to a crisis room as they came off the buses and a memo was immediately sent to staff with what details we knew. No P.A. announcement was made. Rumor control was a must. The Team followed through at the funeral home and funeral. A Building Team was also activated at one of the elementary schools where other siblings attended.

9. There was a traffic fatality late at night that affected the summer school program and driver's education classes. We sent memos, met with students, addressed the driver's ed classes, and were at the funeral home and funeral.

10. This was followed by another homicide of a student that did not greatly affect the educational process (one student), but staff did go to the funeral home and funeral. The one student affected in the summer school program was counseled.

11-12. Two cancer deaths—one last summer and one this spring—were handled in very different manners due to the time of year. For the one in the summer, the staff assisted at the funeral home and funeral. For the one this past spring, Team members counseled students at the high school and junior high (she was a new ninth grader). Members of both staffs attended the funeral home and funeral. A support group is presently running for the close friends of the girl who died in April.

13. The week before school started there was another traffic fatality that was handled immediately by staffing the funeral home and funeral. Upon the opening of school, a large loss and grief support group was established to assist the students in dealing with their grief. The victim had been in an alternative education program for two years and they were a very close group. Since they were all coming to grips with the same death, we allowed the seventeen of them to stay together. (Ordinarily we only have six to eight in such a group.)

14. Ypsilanti Schools house the county POHI (Physically or Otherwise Handicapped Individuals) program. In October of 1987, one of the students from the program was killed by a train as he and friends tried to get off the tracks. His death affected four different school districts. Due to the development of their own plans following ours, each district handled their particular affected students and/or staff.

Modifications

As we have utilized the *Guidelines,* we have found that certain minor modifications were appropriate.

1. We have basically eliminated the P.A. announcement. Instead, we rely on the memo to staff to communicate the facts surrounding the event.
2. The coordination of staff to assist at the funeral home and at the funeral is done by the Team Leader. At the high school, staff familiar with the identified survivors are requested to do an hour or two at the funeral home.
3. Due to the times of notification we have received surrounding several of the events, we have not utilized the staff meeting very often. Since the elementary teachers' reporting time is much earlier than the students, they do meet when necessary.
4. Memorials have been determined by the primary survivors in support groups with monitoring by the group facilitator and approval of the administration. Finalization of a memorial has often signaled that the students were ready to leave group and go on with their lives.
5. Contact with the victim's clergy is also made by the Team Leader. Often the clergy serve as the liaison with the family.

In-Service

To facilitate the implementation of the *Guidelines,* four in-service sessions have been held with more planned for the future. At the first of these in-services, the *Guidelines* were explained and questions were answered. The entire staff of each building was involved. Requests were made for interested volunteers to make themselves known.

The second in-service involved those who said they were interested in being a part of a Building Team. "Possible grief reactions" and the "grieving process" were covered. Techniques were discussed for dealing with the distraught person. The third in-service involved a further breakdown into grade levels to discuss behaviors that may be seen for that age group and subsequent reaction plans were developed. This will be an on-going process.

The fourth in-service session inolved each of the buildings in the district meeting with all of their Team members to plan specific actions within the *Guidelines* for their building. Designations were made as to whom would do what. This same Team and those who help out will meet after each event to debrief and evaluate the way the procedures worked and what might have to be changed next time. This too is an on-going process.

A series of in-service programs are planned to develop specific activities/ lesson plans that will include the following:

1. Personal contact
2. Small groups
3. Class size
4. Assembly information
5. Memorials
6. On-going grief group outlines for each level.

The in-services have allowed us to introduce and then implement the *Guidelines* with some ease. There has been no resistance from staff or administration. When we have needed help from a staff member or administrator, they have been there to support our efforts and give us assistance. This cooperation has been very important to the success of the *Guidelines*. We attribute this success and cooperation in part to the in-service process because we informed them and gave them the opportunity to participate.

Conclusions

The *Guidelines* have proved themselves invaluable to us (Ypsilanti Public Schools). They have enabled us to help individuals and groups through crises while allowing the nonaffected to continue their daily routine without disruption. This is especially important in fairly large schools where a small number can disrupt the educational process of everyone at times. The *Guidelines* have helped us stave off contagion and to minimize additional crises in response to the initial event. For those affected, we have been able to assist them in coping with their feelings in a positive, nonjudgmental manner.

At the high school, we have been able to enlist the support of staff members who know the survivors, not necessarily the victim. This concept was difficult at first to get across. When contacting people to help at the funeral home or funeral, I try to take into consideration who the victim's friends were, what classes they took or activities they were in at school, etc. Stressing that there is nothing at this time that we can do for the victim, I then ask teachers of those students, the survivors, to help "this time." These teachers are the ones best able to relate to the survivors. This procedure has allowed us to incorporate more people into the process and avoided "burning out" any one group of people. The Building Team at the high school has a core of five people—through the preceding process we often have as many as twenty staff involved each time.

Since the *Guidelines* have been in existence, they have not only helped us, but many other school districts and community agencies involved with schools. I have worked with many of the school districts in our area and throughout our state. With assistance from a community mental health group, a county-wide Team and general response plan have been developed to facilitate the handling of crises that may affect many districts at once. This mutual cooperation can also be used in the event of a major disaster in the county whether schools are directly involved or not.

Checklist

This checklist is a guide that can be used with each event. It not only keeps the guesswork out of whether you have done something or not, but allows you to have a record for the future of what you did and what you might want to change next time.

Checklist for Dealing with a Traumatic Event

Event:
1. Contact between Team Leader and Administrator.
   Verification of event_____
                                        with whom
   Details gathered_____
   _____

2. Course of Action
   Need to respond? Yes/No
   Team Leader only_____
   Full Team_____
   Community Resources_____
3. Team Leader notifies Team and/or community resources of meeting:
   Date_____   Time_____   Place_____
4. Administrator and Team Leader meet with Response Team for:
   _____ Briefing of event details
   _____ Course of action planning
   Halls:_____
   Crisis Room(s):_____
                  where

                                      staffing
   _____ Memo preparation
   _____ Memo distributed to all staff
   _____ Determination of need to contact other buildings/districts

   _____ Contact made by_____
5. Team Leader or Administrator contact:
   _____ Family_____   _____
                     name   phone
   _____ Clergy_____   _____
   _____ Funeral Home_____   _____
   Visitations_____   _____
              dates   times
   Funeral_____   _____
           date   time

                                     place
6. Flowers from district/school
7. Scheduling of staff for funeral home/funeral (attach schedule)
8. Need for post-funeral activity for students Yes/No
   If yes,_____   _____
           where   time

   _____
   staff
9. Follow-up
   Student support groups_____
   Memorial_____
   Other_____
10. Debriefing with participating staff and thank you notes to staff.

12

Bereavement Support Groups for Secondary School Students

Grant Baxter, B.Ed and Wendy Stuart, RN

In 1979 the first Bereavement Support Group was held at Lorne Park Secondary School in Mississauga. The group was originally formed in an attempt to meet the needs of students who had suffered a bereavement, and also because the subject matter ideally fitted the purpose of a coping group within a counseling model for a secondary school.

The group was originally formed because of the tragic death of a grade nine student on the GO Train tracks south of the school. His two older sisters were still present in the school grieving his death—their grief acted as a catalyst to bring together the Counseling Services and the school nurse to help these young adolescents.

It was observed that grieving students have a great deal of difficulty concentrating in class, they do not complete homework assignments, and they frequently daydream in class. The end result is that their marks often drop and they fail to complete their courses, which in turn results in tension and disappointment at home.

The school nurse observed depression, insomnia, headaches, weight loss, and physical complaints as symptoms of deeper underlying problems. These young people had all experienced the loss of a family member or close friend through death (some cases, suicide). Each student reacted to the death differently but all seemed to be in need of some support through the grieving process. It was decided that a bereavement support group might be the answer for these young people.

Identification of grieving students can be accomplished with the following methods. Students are tracked through attendance, by notes sent from home excusing students for a funeral. Students inform teachers of deaths of friends and these names are forwarded to Counseling Services and kept on file. Feeder schools are requested to submit names for their incoming bereaved grade 9 students, and tragic or violent deaths in the community are usually reported through the media. In the case of life-threatening illnesses the school is sometimes contacted by the hospital social work department; these students can be counseled before the death occurs, either through the school nurse, counseling services, or even a peer counselor.

The basic goals for forming support groups are to first acknowledge the bereaved student and to provide emotional support during the academic year. The groups provide acceptance and understanding of the grief process by introducing students to other students in similar circumstances. The group leaders act as liaison between students and staff and assist students to specifically identify problems that can be solved by using a variety of techniques.

Group sessions are held once a week for approximately 10 to 12 weeks. Sessions are held during school hours and end at the conclusion of the school day. This allows "extra" time for any session and gives students "recovery time" so that they do not have to return to classes. All sessions should be held in a private room free from interruptions. Before students are invited to join the groups, a pre-intake interview is arranged with both leaders. During this session the bereavement is recognized and such issues as time and place, confidentiality, guidelines concerning group participation and the sharing of ideas are discussed. This process starts the beginning of group cohesiveness by developing trust and rapport with the student.

It is always emphasized that these groups are support groups rather than therapy groups and that helping the grieving teen is the main focus of the group. Most problems initiated by group members revolve around the themes of guilt, anger, feelings of loneliness, nightmares, depression, thoughts of suicide, and communication problems at home and at school.

Communication during bereavement is always difficult and the inability of parents to talk about the death because of their own emotions is disturbing to young people who often feel left out or abandoned during this time. This is particularly evident in the case of suicides where siblings are sometimes denied the facts surrounding the death. For example, if the surviving parent remains home and becomes housebound, the student feels they must now keep the grieving parent happy, and in so doing feel they must curtail their own social life. The student then becomes angry because their social life is curtailed.

Many times the surviving parent enters into a new relationship too soon after the death of a partner. Such relationships often cause problems because of reorganization of household rules or inclusion of new siblings in the household. Sometimes because of financial obligations drastic changes in life-style occur and changes of friends, schools, status, and physical relocations must be dealt with by the teenager. In some cases the parent turns to alcohol or drugs because he or she cannot deal effectively with the death of the deceased partner. Teenagers are sometimes faced with or are asked to participate in the legal details and problems of disputed wills. The teenager must then, often suddenly, assume the parent role in order to protect his own interests.

Students are often upset by the occurrence of unusual visual hallucinations. For example, a student in her bedroom saw her deceased father standing at the foot of her bed—he calmly reassured her that he was not unhappy. At the time of the hallucination she smelled earth. This both reassured and frightened her. Another student who was referred after psychiatric intervention, continued to have horrible nightmares depicting her father dying his terrible death through fire, his flesh being burned from his body. She felt supported by the group who listened and empathized with her, and reassured her that she was not going insane. The group also had practical suggestions as to how she could deal with these nightmares.

Another problem related by young people is the hero worship syndrome on behalf of their parents. The deceased's siblings room is out-of-bounds and becomes a shrine that cannot be altered or disturbed. Parents often "forget" the usual tensions surrounding teenage life and the deceased becomes a hero whom the surviving siblings are encouraged to emulate.

A re-occurring theme is lack of concentration around scholastic endeavors. A drop in grades usually leads to further tension at home—the surviving parent can usually cope with the world of work because it is "routine" but a student must remain a student, e.g., study, learn new material, and reproduce it for examinations and quizzes. Since all grieving students find concentrating extremely difficult, helping the student and parent to recognize this fact lessens the pressure at home and in turn leads to improved communication at home.

All grieving students express feelings of anger and think of suicide. This is best illustrated by a student whose parents were killed in a motor vehicle accident only yards from home. As a result he had to move away from home, school, friends, leave his dog, and come to live with his older brother and his wife and children. The young driver who killed his parents received a "light sentence." He remarked that justice had not been done and that the Toronto Blue Jay who killed a seagull with a baseball received a "heavier" fine. Many adolescents express anger toward hospital and ambulance personnel because they feel that more treatment could have been administered—this leads to difficulties with medical personnel if further therapy is required at a later date. Most students have suicidal feelings sometime during the grieving process. Upon sharing of this information group leaders should institute a suicide assessment check with each member of the group. In most cases adolescents do not wish to die but merely to alleviate the pain of grieving.

It is hoped that throughout the sessions group members will be allowed the opportunity to work through normal grief reactions. It should also be pointed out that not all group sessions are of a heavy emotional nature. Often, humorous anecdotes relieve the tension and many problems that are brought to the group can be solved.

The timing and method of ending the group are especially delicate matters. A group lunch is usually arranged, followed by a last session of evaluation and closing. Every student has a chance to bring any unfinished business to the group. Each group member is asked to write an evaluation and these are read confidentially by the group leaders. Each group member is also guaranteed continual contact with the group leaders and other members of the group. Group members often take advantage of this available contact especially on the anniversary of the death, or at other times when flashbacks or other stressful situations are experienced. Group members are never abandoned. They have both leader contact and peer counselor contact. Members of previous groups have often been used successfully as peer counselors in dealing with life-threatening illnesses involving family members. They provide excellent support for students who have lost a parent before being admitted to a group.

In closing, both authors feel it is extremely important that group facilitators possess some training in group process and bereavement counseling.

The process of bereavement counseling has proved extremely valuable as a method of group counseling. It is a learning and growth experience for both the group members and the group facilitators. We believe that such groups should be part of any dynamic counseling program as they offer a direct service to secondary school students.

13

Teen Suicide: Sources, Signals, and Prevention

Robert G. Stevenson, EdD

The topic of adolescent suicide is clearly a difficult one to face. We act as though life is "fair" and the future "predictable" but most of us know that this is not the case. Reality can be summed up in a currently popular bumper sticker which states succinctly, Shit Happens. We can never predict the future with certainty and things happen around us that are by no means fair. We might paraphrase that bumper sticker by saying that Death Happens and that it often happens in tragic circumstances.

The forcible loss of someone or something precious creates a condition known as bereavement. Grief is the process by which one recovers from that bereavement. The "normal" grief process involves both emotional and physical discomfort. It can last for a year or more and young people have the ability to delay this process for up to five years. Even this "normal" grief process, which is experienced by survivors of any bereavement, carries links to suicide. The major emotions present in most grief reactions are helplessness, hopelessness, and loneliness. These are three of the four emotions present in many suicide attempts. The only major one missing is worthlessness and this feeling is present for many of today's young people. Clearly many of these young people are "at risk." Those who wish to help these young people are seeking answers to many questions:

— What is suicide?
— How great is the risk for today's young people?
— Why do people commit suicide?
— What information can provide clues to alert others?
— How can a "nonprofessional" be of help?
— How is death by suicide different from other deaths?

125

— What can be done to help survivors of suicide?

This chapter will offer information that can serve as a starting point for individuals seeking answers to each of these questions.

Information and Misinformation

Throughout this discussion, suicide will be defined as the "taking" of one's own life, as opposed to sacrificing it. This is an important distinction to make for young people who sometimes see suicide as heroic and experience the mixed feelings of sadness and admiration one might associate with the death of a soldier who threw himself onto a grenade to save his comrades. Also, deaths by suicide are referred to as "completed" suicide attempts and not as "successful" suicides. The idea that someone who has died because he/she could no longer face the problems of living should never be referred to as a success. This use of success has long been standard practice in the literature on suicide, but if it causes even one young person to view those still alive after an attempt as "failures" and to act on that view, how could it be justified?

Descriptions of suicides have been recorded since biblical times, but the man who first used a systematic approach in examining data about suicide was Emile Durkheim. Durkheim, known as the Father of Sociology because of his use of the scientific method with the social sciences, produced a study that is still used as a reference today (Durkheim 1950). We now have many statistics dealing with suicide, but they do not, by themselves answer our next question: How great a problem is suicide for today's young people? How Great Is The Risk?

Parents of high school students who are told that their children are eight times more likely to die in a suicide attempt than junior high or middle school students would believe that the danger is both grave and immediate. The actual number of deaths is about 1 per 100,000 among young people ages 10–14 years of age and 8 per 100,000 among those 15–19. The numbers alone make the danger appear far less immediate. However, there are over 400,000 suicide attempts by adolescents annually (Greenberg 1985) and every completed suicide may leave literally thousands of survivors in its wake. A survivor of suicide is one who is alive after a loved one (or a person with whom they identified) has died as the result of a completed suicide. The effect of media coverage and word of mouth among peers following the 5,000 deaths by suicide that occur among adolescents annually may place as many as two to five million teens at greater risk of a suicide attempt themselves. The statistics of adolescent suicide may generate greater governmental concern or promote greater funding for suicide prevention programs, but caring adults should only need to know that the problem exists and that if our knowledge can help prevent even one life from being ended prematurely the time and effort expended to acquire it will have been worthwhile.

When and Where do Attempts Occur?

Generally we can say that adolescents attempt suicide in greater numbers on weekends between midnight and sunrise, and on weekdays during school hours. Attempts occur most frequently at home and in growing numbers in or near school. However, this has little or no meaning when speaking of a specific individual. The important fact to remember then is that the place of a suicide attempt is determined by the individual person. Just when a person may feel that he/she has no control over life, they are still exercising control, only they are often unaware of it.

Adolescents at risk of a suicide attempt do not present as clear a profile as many adults do. A defiant, active youth may feel consumed by anger, by a "wish to kill," and then turn that anger inward in a suicide attempt. A compliant, passive teen may feel unable to live with the guilt they feel and succumb to a "wish to be killed." A high achiever, devoid of anger or guilt and showing all the external signs of success may seek to escape this pressure (whether internal or external) by acting upon a wish to die. The decision to act on this "wish" may last for only a short period of time. It may be no longer than a few minutes. Freud's model of opposing drives for life (Eros) and death (Thanatos) that are in competition within each individual is useful in trying to understand this period of crisis. For the individual considering suicide, suicide is not a problem . . . it is a solution. It is something else, some other problem, which has brought the person to the point where suicide is seen in this manner. If an adolescent can be pulled through this crisis period, it is possible that, with help to solve the problem that brought them to this point, such a crisis need not reoccur.

It is this point that gives suicide prevention programs much of their impetus. One piece of information or one caring individual could tip the balance in favor of life and away from death. After all, in most cases, it is not that the person wishes to "be dead" but to be relieved of some pressure, some pain, some problem that they can no longer face. The pain has caused the person to focus larger and larger amounts of time and energy solely on the present so that it becomes hard and then impossible to see a better future, or to be aware of the needs and feelings of others.

Why Do People Commit Suicide?

Generally, suicide attempts come as the result of a sudden loss of hope, a failure of communication, impulse, or serious illness. The loss of hope can occur after an event that appears small to others (a missed appointment, a job setback, a family argument), but was for the individual the "straw that broke the camel's back." The failure of communication takes place in situations where there were people all around who "could have" or "would have" helped if they had only known, but somehow no one realized how bad things were for the person in their midst. Impulse is no longer understood in the way it once was. Now, instead of a sudden, unpredictable act, the suicide is seen as an action that may have been a long time in contemplation or even preparation, but that was seen as "sudden" by others when it was finally acted out. Serious illness becomes a factor when an individual chooses "quality" over "quantity" of life. The person decides that how well he or she lives is more important than how long the life is.

Adolescents face additional pressures beyond those listed above. They are in the midst of a period of physical and biochemical change. Their bodies are changing so rapidly, with accompanying mood swings, that at times they feel as if they are on an emotional roller coaster. Any use of alcohol or drugs will only make the highs higher, the lows lower, and increase the frequency as well as the intensity of the mood shifts.

Adolescence is a period of intense self-examination. Adolescents set aside many of the checks and balances (family, school, religion) that previously placed automatic limits on their behavior. They may well embrace these standards at some future date, but they first want to examine each and see if this is a standard they personally are willing to accept. In trying to gain more control over their own lives, they are disengaging the "brakes" just as their emotions appear to be running away with them.

Adolescence is also a time of emerging sexuality. Sexual activity and abstinence can each cause self-doubt, uncertainty, or guilt. However, an even greater issue for many adolescents is the need to come to terms with their own sexuality. How does one become a complete person without running the risk of becoming like some of the parodies of real people that bombard young people in the media and in real life every day? It is a task that many adults have yet to complete in middle age and to expect it of teens is expecting a great deal indeed.

The last issue is perhaps the most important task facing adolescents. They must cut parental ties based on a relationship of dependence and re-form them on a basis of greater equality. The process can be as painful and confusing for adolescents as it often is for parents. As teens desire the freedom to take greater control of their lives, they miss the lost security of youth and mourn that loss.

Faced with all of this uncertainty, the need to learn new roles and to build a place for themselves in an uncertain world, while feeling all of the frustration and emotional pain that adolescence can bring, each teen must also be able to put up with the well-meaning adults who bombard them with platitudes such as the ever-popular, "These are the best years of your life!" When we look at all that is expected of young people, along with the demands of school and career, is it so surprising that some young people find such "reassurances" a scary thought?

A plethora of scholarly articles presenting new, and sometimes conflicting, research about adolescents and the growing number of youth suicides can seem overwhelming to the nonprofessional. What caring adults want is a way to identify young people who may need help, and a knowledge of how to offer that help or where to go to find others who can.

Clues to a Potential Suicide

There are so many helpful lists that identify warning signs of a potential suicide that they would literally fill this book. Some of the more widely used lists are those of Hunt (1988), Allen (1986), Harold (1984), Rickgarn (1983), Stevenson (1980), and Ritter (1978). There is no one source for helpful information, or one best list. The following list draws on the points mentioned in many of these previous works.

—*A previous attempt.* Most young people who die as the result of a completed suicide have made a previous attempt.

—*A pattern of behavior causing "self-injury" (including the abuse of drugs, alcohol, tobacco).* A suicide attempt may well be the next step in such a pattern.

—*Talking about suicide (except for the very young).* Most adolescent suicide attempters spoke of their situation and/or their thoughts of suicide before making an actual attempt. The seriousness of the situation is often concealed in "humor."

—*Loss of appetite, weight, interest in life (friends, school, dating, work, or hobbies).* These may be signs of *apathy*, the emotional withdrawal of a person from life. This emotional withdrawal may be preliminary to a permanent physical withdrawal through suicide.

—*Sudden calm after a long or deep period of depression.* This "calm" may come from the certain knowledge that the person's pain will soon be ended permanently.

—*Giving away possessions.* This can be a cry for help, but does not occur as frequently as we might be led to believe by recent popular television shows and films.

—*Obtaining the means.* The purchase of a weapon, collecting pills, etc. may be overlooked by caring relatives or friends who cannot bear to face the possible implications of such actions.

—*Creative works that show recurrent themes of depression, death or "pressure."* These writings, poems, drawings, or other works of art may provide the young person with a way of expressing feelings and thoughts that are too frightening to be put into words.

—*A sudden change in almost any recurring pattern of behavior.* Most of the points listed above should be seen as part of a pattern of behaviors and not viewed in isolation. When a pattern of behavior changes, it is always wise to look for a reason before such changes are simply assigned to growing pains.

How Can a Non-Professional Be of Help?

Persons considering suicide often confide in someone else. This person, referred to as a gatekeeper, is usually a friend or stranger rather than a person who is seen as an authority figure. This confidence gives the person a chance to "test" the reality of the situation and to consider aloud the effects of "suicidal" thoughts prior to an actual attempt. The gatekeeper is so named because the confidence of the person contemplating suicide has made this individual the one who, for him or her, stands at the gate between life and death and holds the key that can open that gate or help to keep it closed.

Adolescents are most likely to place a friend or acquaintance in the position of gatekeeper. For that reason, adolescents should be equipped with some facts on which to base their actions. A person in the position of gatekeeper should remember the following points:

NEVER	ALWAYS
—NEVER dismiss a threat or underestimate it. The person may make an attempt to convince others of the seriousness of his/her intent.	—ALWAYS take all comments or threats seriously. When looking at the possible consequences of an error, it is the safest course. To be needlessly concerned could mean one more source of aggravation, but to fail to express concern could contribute to a death.
—NEVER try to shock or challenge the person. It may bring about the very activity you are trying to avoid.	—ALWAYS assume that this person *must* live. Uncertainty on the part of gatekeepers can weaken resolve and limit their ability to be of help.
—NEVER offer analysis to the person. He or she doesn't need the situation to be labeled by others while the problem remains. However, *do* assess the immediate likelihood of this person acting on these thoughts and feel	—ALWAYS be genuine, strong, interested, and stable. This is no time for a display of insincere emotion, or to make the person guilty for sharing this burden with you.

ings to estimate the present danger, but keep this to yourself.

—NEVER promise total confidentiality. This is a demand made by some people as a condition for sharing information. Instead of agreeing before understanding the consequences, state that you will maintain confidentiality unless there is reason to believe that this silence might result in injury to someone.

—NEVER argue the pros and cons of suicide. This is perhaps the most common error. The gatekeeper usually intends to reinforce reasons against suicide while minimizing the problems that made it a possibility. There are two reasons why this course of action is too dangerous to risk. The first is that people in need of help will quite probably be using "selective perception." They see only part of what is there or view it from a different perspective. They may well focus only on the negatives in such a list, or may view "positive" items as negatives. Also, by even starting such a list, you confirm that there are times when suicide might be the correct course of action, otherwise why would one even start such a project. This might be just the validation needed by someone already considering suicide as a way of solving a problem.

—NEVER assume that time heals all wounds. Anniversaries of losses can renew feelings of pain and helplessness, and the passage of time without resolution of a problem may be seen only as a confirmation of hopelessness.

—ALWAYS be firm with the person. If you believe that something must be done (such as seeking professional help) tell the person, don't ask them what they think. Having to make one more decision may only add to the pressure they are already under.

—ALWAYS listen to the person's story. Really listen to what they are saying before you worry about what you will say when the person stops talking.

—AlWAYS be willing to ask questions. Two of the most important questions are: "Is this the worst it has ever been for you?" and "Are you thinking of hurting yourself (suicide)?" When asked if they have been thinking about suicide, people who have are often relieved to answer honestly. To ask if this is "the worst it has been" can give important insight to a person at risk if the answer is "Yes."

—ALWAYS be willing to seek professional help if possible. Admitting that someone needs professional help from a doctor, therapist, or counselor is not a sign of weakness. We should be willing to draw on professional talent to help people as easily as we would call upon a mechanic for our cars. The "stigma" associated with mental health counseling must be relegated to the past. No friends or family need to bear this responsibility alone.

The Role of the School

The problems faced by teens do not exist in isolation. In looking at the environment of young people, the school is the second most important factor in the lives of teens; only the family is more important. The willingness of growing numbers of educators to become involved in efforts to help troubled teens is a source of hope for the future. The first step in this involvement is a willingness to talk about the problems that exist and that may contribute to suicide.

It is most often true that talking about a problem does not make the problem worse. It can help by allowing people to feel "control" over the situation. Words we cannot say, for whatever reason, control us. Saying those words aloud restores control to people , where it belongs. Also, talking can provide a beneficial catharsis and may help a person to arrive at new solutions for old problems.

Silence reinforces helplessness and increases feelings of guilt and anger. Hardly a day goes by that young people don't learn of teen suicide attempts or see the results of a completed suicide splashed through the media. If the adults around them do nothing, it may well show them that there is nothing that can be said or done . . . they are helpless. If there are things that could be done and we still do or say nothing it may be because these young people do not deserve help or that we simply choose not to help. The resulting feelings of guilt (at not being worth helping) or anger (at our apparent decision not to help) can have far-reaching consequences not the least of which is building a sense of worthlessness—one of the key emotions present in suicide attempts.

Peer Listeners—Breaking the Silence

Many schools have begun training students to help their peers. Details of the programs vary, but all involve the willingness of students to take the time to listen to others who feel a need to talk. That may be all that is needed, or a referral to available professionals may follow, but peer listening has shown itself to be an effective first step in stemming the destructive tide of adolescent self-destruction. Teens are willing to help, but there must be responsible adult leadership to help those teens with the role they have chosen to play. The peer listeners have become an important support group for fellow students. Faculty advisors are the support network for those peer listeners themselves.

Teens and staff need a regular system of support and a knowledge of the sources of help and the procedures for obtaining it. Administrators, board members, and parents can become involved in creating a positive climate for such peer programs. Acknowledging the positive role that such a program can play helps everyone involved to feel they are asserting control over their own lives by carrying out their part in building the positive sense of "community" that can counteract a feeling of isolation and loneliness.

The growing wave of criticism by groups opposed to suicide prevention programs (such as the Eagle Forum) must be faced and answered. Suicide prevention programs must always be reevaluated so that they can be strengthened and improved in their work. For this reason critics always will have an important place. However, the criticism now appearing from the Eagle Forum seeks not to improve these programs designed to help young people, but to end them with a barrage of unverified conclusions, exaggerations, and half-truths. Parents and educators must cooperate and not allow extremists to divide us as we all attempt to help the young people for whom we care.

Jack Kent, in *There's No Such Thing As A Dragon,* tells of one family's dragon that grew larger as each family member denied its existence. Acknowledging that it was there put it back into perspective. Suicide is todays dragon. With a conspiracy of silence it can grow. The question then is, how big do we want this dragon to be?

Loss and Suicide

As was mentioned above, the "normal" grief process involves both emotional and physical discomfort and its emotions (helplessness, hopelessness, and loneliness) can seem overwhelming. Grief can last for a year or more—some young people can postpone it for up to five years. Even this normal grief process, which is experienced by the survivors of any death, carries links to suicide. Helplessness, hopelessness, and loneliness are three of the four emotions present in many suicide attempts. The only major one missing is *worthlessness* and this feeling is present in many survivors of suicide. The aftermath of suicide is "different" from other types of bereavement for those left behind. The reasons for this difference are complex; some of them are found in the manner of death, some in the reactions of individuals, and some in the history and culture that influence the reaction of society. An understanding of the nature of a death by suicide is essential for those who wish to help the survivors.

CHARACTERISTICS OF A DEATH BY SUICIDE

It is Sudden and Seldom Anticipated.   Sudden loss is more likely to complicate the grief process than a death that is anticipated—even after prolonged suffering. Sudden death may be "kinder" to the deceased but it exacts a greater toll on the survivors.

In retrospect one may question how others could have failed to see the suffering in a person that led to a suicide. However, the anxiety that the suffering of a loved one causes in others makes it hard for those concerned individuals, such as parents or siblings, to "see" that suffering in the one they care about. It is affection and not indifference which blinds them to the suffering of the individual.

It is Often Violent.   Even where there is not a violent death, a suicide violently rips apart our ideas concerning the natural order of things.

It Takes Place in the Presence of Other Stresses.   For those considering suicide, it is not a "problem" but a "solution." In most cases, there were already other problems existing before the suicide attempt. These problems have an impact on survivors as well and will often complicate grieving.

It Accentuates Feelings of Regret and Guilt in the Survivors.   Survivors use hindsight to see "signs" of possible suicide and constantly say "If only . . ." or "What if . . ." as they replay past events. What we believe to be true can be more important than reality. The silence imposed on survivors can aggravate these feelings.

Survivors Experience a Feeling of Loss of "Control."   This feeling can cause an inability to act, creating even greater loss of control—a "classic" negative feedback loop. A coping style of "submission," similar to the model used by Gullo (1984) is often adopted by the survivors.

Loss of Control is Reinforced by a Flood of Emotions.   Anger, sadness, apathy (withdrawing from life), and regrets may be experienced in waves or simultaneously. This places greater demands on those who interact with survivors.

Grief can be Complicated by Reactions of Society. Support systems often disappear. Rituals are sometimes withheld. The media can play a significant role in shaping the reactions of a community, whether positive or negative.

Survivors Become Isolated by the "Distancing" of Others. Communications break down as survivors see others as "judgmental" by their silence and other remain silent about the suicide because they believe survivors will be overly sensitive.

Humor is often used as a way of approaching a topic that cannot be discussed in the usual manner. Reactions that appear to be inappropriate should be examined to help the individuals who display them, but that does not mean that they are any less painful for the survivors to experience. In an attempt to regain feelings of control, labels may be applied to the deceased to stress the way(s) in which he or she was different from those applying the label or from their friends. This person is said to have died because he/she was a "loser," or "loner," or "problem" of some sort. Labeling may be seen as helpful by "outsiders" but it can exact a terrible toll on survivors.

Finally, some deaths that are not suicides are now being labeled as such by people who find this an easier death to cope with, even though family members object strongly. Auto-erotic deaths have produced this reaction. "Control" over the situation through descriptions and labels again is taken by society at the expense of family members—who may desperately wish to face the reality of what took place.

Even When Most of The Above Do Not Occur, Survivors May Still Believe Them to Be True. Just as there may have been options that the deceased could not see, survivors may believe that all possible negative reactions are taking place, even when they are not.

The history of society's treatment of survivors, or an examination of the possible coping behaviors of individuals, would perhaps be interesting at this point. However, an excellent discussion of this material is available elsewhere (Dunne et al. 1987). As an educator, I believe what is needed is a plan or set of guidelines so that we can take a step toward lessening the negative impact of a suicide on survivors. The following guidelines are by no means a definitive protocol. They may, however, be used as a starting point in anticipating our response when a suicide occurs.

Helping the Survivors of Suicide: Guidelines For Educators and Parents

When a completed suicide occurs, the following steps have been found useful:

Talk About It.   Talking about a problem can help to clarify our thoughts and feelings. When we can't speak of an issue, the words control us but when we do speak of it we experience greater feelings of control.

Explain the Facts as You Know Them and Answer All Rumors.   After a loss we seek information as a way of feeling in control, stories are spread rapidly, many of them untrue. Stopping rumors helps to avoid unnecessary additional pain. Providing factual information establishes a relationship of trust that will be helpful in the future.

Promote Positive Attitudes and Positive Solutions.   Suicide has been called a permanent solution to a temporary problem. Stress the positive ways of solving problems or of enduring the pain that follows a loss. Do not try to deal with problems and concerns immediately unless the student wishes to discuss this topic. When the groundwork has been laid by stressing the positive aspects of the person's life, it will then be time to face the problems directly. This is a variation of a method used with potentially suicidal individuals.

Acknowledge the Change(s) This Death Has Caused But Do Not Validate the Suicide.   "Change" is a word that describes the reality of the situation and avoids negative implications. It allows the situation to be discussed in a nonjudgmental way. Discuss how things have changed for the survivor. Remember that each person is an individual with a unique perspective on what has happened and on how it will effect him/her. Do not attempt to present the deceased as "better off" because this sort of well-intentioned but meaningless platitude may produce enough anger to block any further attempts to help. Also, as was stressed earlier, do not attempt to weigh the "pros and cons" of the situation.

Do Not "Romanticize" But Do Commemorate the Death.   Suicide clusters are a concern, but the messages we give by doing nothing may be far worse than the impact of anything we do. To do nothing can cause feelings of helplessness, hopelessness, and worthlessness. A Pennsylvania high school recently canceled graduation exercises because of threats by students who were angered by the failure of the school to have any commemoration (or even mention) of the death of a student by suicide. The school chose silence but the reactions of the students, extreme as they seemed, quickly subsided after they had a visible change in routine. They had forced a commemoration after all. Having a protocol in place to use after every death of a member of the school community (regardless of how) has been found to be an effective way of forestalling such drastic actions (Stevenson and Powers 1987).

Help Survivors to Remember the "Complete" Individual. No one is all bad or all good. After a suicide there is a tendency among some survivors to portray the deceased in one extreme or the other. It is impossible to grieve the real person who died while wrapped up in a mental image of someone who never really existed in that way at all.

Record Dates of Deaths So That There Can Be a Special Vigilance on "Anniversaries." Survivors are at special risk on the anniversary of a loss. Staff should be aware of the extra pressures that can effect the person at such a time.

Take Time to Help the Helpers. The time to plan for this type of event is *before* it occurs. Staff members are also survivors. There must also be a way for staff to deal with their own feelings and reactions.

Conclusion

When any tragedy strikes many questions are raised; the most urgent is the need to know *why* this thing happened. Sometimes the why of a suicide will never be known. However, the need to have this question answered is so strong that we may seize on any available answer, regardless of whether or not it is the right one, mistaking a correlation for a cause-effect relationship.

Rock music has served as the answer for some people. A young boy who died from a completed suicide was found to have a music cassette in his pocket. One of the songs on the tape spoke of suicide (through alcohol abuse). The headline in a major New Jersey newspaper blared out "Edison Boy Kills Himself; Had Rock Tape On Suicide" (*The Record* April 26, 1988). For many, that headline was all the information they needed. Had he been listening to the tape? What other things did he have in his possession? What problems may have led him to that point? Why was music singled out in that way? The local prosecutor had mentioned music as one thing that plays a role in the lives of young people and merely mentioned the tape as a way of saying that parents should try to be aware of all the factors that influence the lives of their children. The job is huge, but children deserve our best efforts to do it. That was not the message that came through the press as follow-up articles featured the efforts of people to censor music lyrics and to have warnings printed on album covers—as though the issue of cause and effect were already settled. Dr. Hannelore Wass (1988) of the University of Florida is, with the assistance of educators across the country, conducting a series of studies of preferences for rock music, especially those with themes of homicide, suicide, or violence. Months of effort have still not produced evidence of the clear cause and effect relationship seen by that headline writer. The quick indictment of rock music shows a benefit of prejudice; namely, the ability to make up one's mind without knowing the facts.

Another easy target on which to blame the rise in youth suicide comes in the form of suicide prevention and/or death education programs. In northern New Jersey, to combat the growing number of adolescent suicides, the schools of Bergen County implemented a program known as A.S.A.P. (the Adolescent Suicide Awareness Program). It was developed at River Dell Regional High School by the staff of the South Bergen Mental Health Center (Ryerson and Acocella 1984). By the end of 1984, almost every high school in the service area of the mental health center had also implemented sections of this program. The number of completed adolescent suicides in the county declined steadily for four straight years. In 1987, there were five completed youth suicides, four of which occurred at one time in one of the few towns that chose not to implement this program. This number was still lower than it had been in the years before the program was begun.

The death education program at River Dell School in Oradell has been taught within the social studies department since 1972. Over 1200 students have completed the elective course, originally nine weeks and now a full semester in length. There have been no completed suicides among those students and only one made a suicide attempt, which came years after high school graduation. Several students had made suicide attempts before taking the course and at least twenty students gave written testimonials to their belief that the course had helped them avoid a repetition of their past action. One student wrote to the instructor, ". . . last night, looking at my notebook and thinking about what was said in class saved my life. I owe you one . . . a BIG one . . . maybe two or three!"

These examples will not dissuade the critics who "know" that suicide prevention is beyond the scope of educators. Belief in the benefits of such programs is not simply "trendy" as Phyllis Schlafly (1987) would have us believe, but can play a vital role in fulfilling the mandate given to our public schools to educate the "whole" child. Excess anger and anxiety are known to block effective communication. The critics of suicide prevention programs have increased both anxiety and anger. They seek to play upon the anxiety of parents who are only trying to provide a good life for their children and are afraid that they may not be doing a good enough job. They exude anger at a school system which they see as ignoring them simply because it does not agree with their often unfounded conclusions. Hopefully, concerned parents and educators will be able to combine their efforts and move past the anger and anxiety to develop a rational plan to help our young people address this vital issue. An adversarial relationship will help no one. A cooperative effort to find the best course of action will benefit all. We cannot make our kids "suicide proof," but if we work together the result could be to make them "suicide resistant." That is enough reason for all this effort on their behalf.

References

Allen, R. 1986 *Teen suicide prevention.* Washington: Teen Suicide Prevention Task Force.

Dunne, E.J., J.L. McIntosh, and K. Dunne-Maxim ed. 1987. *Suicide and its aftermath: Understanding and counseling the survivors.* New York: Norton.

Durkheim, E. 1950. *The suicide.* (trans. Spalding). New York City: Free Press.

Greenberg, R. 1985. Adolescent suicide. *Psychiatry Letter* December, 69–70.

Gullo, S.V. and E.H. Plimpton. 1985. On understanding and coping with death during childhood. In *Death and Children: A Guide for educators, parents and caregivers.* New York: Tappan.

Harold, M. 1984. Counselors fight suicide plague. *Guideposts* December 6, 1–6.

Hunt, C. 1988. The tree of life: Warning signs of suicide. In M. Christopher, *Taking action against suicide.* Forecast April, pp. 19.

Kent, J. 1975. *There's no such thing as a dragon.* New York: Golden.

Peck, M.L., N.L. Farberow and R.E. Litman ed. 1985. *Youth Suicide.* New York: Springer.

Pfeffer, C.R. 1986. *The suicidal child.* New York: Guilford Press.

Rickgarn, R.L. 1983. *The issue is: Suicide.* Minneaplois: University of Minnesota.

Ritter, C. 1978. Suicide: The deadly signals. *The Plain Truth* February: 25–27, 44.

Ryerson, D.M. and F.G. Acocella. 1984. Recognizing and preventing the self-destructive behavior of adolescents. *Educational Viewpoints* Fall: 10–13.

Schlafly, P. 1988 Death education comes into open. *Brooklyn Spectator,* April 13.

Schowalter, J.E., R.G. Stevenson, et. al. 1987. *Children and death: Perspectives from birth through adolescence.* New York: Praeger.

Stevenson, R.G. 1980. Teenage suicide. *The Jamie Schuman Center Newsletter* October: 3–4.

Stevenson, R.G. and H.L. Powers. 1987. How to handle death in the school. *The Education Digest* May: 42–43.

Wass, H. 1988. Adolescents and destructive themes in rock music. Paper delivered at King's College, London, Ontario, May 31.

14

Suicide Postvention in School Systems: A Model

Antoon A. Leenaars, PhD, C.Psych
and Susanne Wenckstern, MA

Postvention is a term introduced by Shneidman (1973, 1981, 1983). It refers to the following:

> Those things done after the dire event has occurred that serve to mollify the after affects of the event in a person who has attempted suicide, or to deal with the adversé effects as the survivor-victims of a person who has committed suicide (Shneidman 1973, p.385).

Postvention is offering mental health services to the bereaved survivors. It includes service to all survivors who are in need—children, parents, teachers, friends, etc. Shneidman has frequently noted that the development of suicide (and death) postvention will be important future endeavors. School systems will be a critical force in these efforts with our young people.

This chapter, presenting a model for suicide postvention in schools, is divided into four major sections and a brief concluding remark. The first section provides a frame to see suicide as a trauma, a catastrophe—post-traumatic stress. The second is a review of the scant literature; the third is an outline of our model, based on Schneidman's insights on postvention. The fourth major section provides a number of case examples.

Post-Traumatic Stress

Suicide is a trauma for the survivors. Our own experience with such survivors— in schools and other systems—suggests that this type of bereavement is associ-

The authors wish to thank the Windsor Board of Education in their support of our effort. J. Lin has contributed significantly to the program itself. Discussions with Dr. E. Shneidman are greatly appreciated. The views expressed in this chapter are the authors' and not necesarily those of the Windsor Board of Education.

ated with a prolonged stress response in many individuals. Research supports this view (Gleser, Green and Wignet 1981; Horowitz 1979). Wilson, Smith, and Johnson (1985) have reported that loss of a significant other, including by suicide, results in significant stress; indeed, the greater the degree of loss and/ or its symbolic implication (such as might be experienced in relation to a previous death), the more severe is the stress syndrome. Freud in 1917 (b) already noted that loss of an object (related primarily to attachment) results in trauma with symptoms of depression. Indeed, from his clinical records, he had noted that the greater the degree of loss, the greater the stress. It would appear from our view that this is especially true for suicide since more than any other death in our society, there is a social (and often personal dynamic) stigma for the survivors. We personally believe that it is heuristic to view this event from the post-trauma stress disorder framework.

The literature on victims of traumatic events is comprised of more or less distinct areas (Janoff-Bulman 1985). This is certainly true for suicide. Often suicide is not even discussed in bereavement texts. Yet there are common psychological experiences. Recognition of the commonalities has recently been furthered by the American Psychiatric Association's (APA's) DSM-III (1980). In this diagnostic manual, there is a new classification—the post-traumatic stress disorder (PTSD)—that spells out characteristic symptoms that may follow "a psychologically traumatic event that is generally outside the range of usual human experience." PTSD is most often associated with military combat, particularly victims of the Vietnam War (Figley 1978). As Janoff-Bulman (1985) points out, PTSD can be associated with other traumatic events; e.g., serious crimes, accidents, disasters. Suicide is clearly outside the usual human experience. It, indeed, evokes "significant symptoms of distress in most people" (Leenaars 1988; Shneidman 1985).

Traumatic stress disorder refers to those natural behaviors and emotions that occur during a catastrophe. Figley (1985) defined post-traumatic stress disorder (PTSD) "as a set of conscious and unconscious behaviours and emotions associated with dealing with the memories of the stressors of the catastrophe and immediately afterwards." In addition to the existence of a recognized stressor, PTSD, as defined by the PA's manual, includes the following: reexperiencing of the trauma (e.g., recurrent recollection, recurrent dreams, associations that the event is recurring); numbing of responsiveness to a reduced involvement with external world (e.g., diminished interest, detachment, constricted affect); and at least two of the following symptoms: hyperalertness, sleep disturbance, survivor guilt, problem in memory/concentration, avoidance of events that evoke recall, intensification of symptoms by events that symbolize events.

Our own experience with survivors of suicide would suggest that many would fit such a description. Although few of us (with the exception of police, hospital staff, firemen, guards), will, for example, ever experience finding "a body," one only has to imagine what it would be like for a father to find his son dead by a gunshot wound to his head, the boy's brains and blood all over the wall. Or imagine a student killing himself in front of his classmates Or a guard cutting down a body, trying to provide resuscitation. For them, the likelihood of experiencing PTSD is high; however, even the information about a suicide can evoke a response, evident by the contagion effect. A few years ago in Japan, an 18-year-old pop idol, Yukiko Okada, after a fight with her lover, leaped to her death from the building that housed her recording company in Tokyo. In the 17 days following her suicide, the suicide toll reached 33 young people. Phillips (1986; April 1986) has recently documented that teenage (and adult) clusters do exist. The authors vividly recall a number of cases in our local school system. One young man—who clearly exhibited PTSD—four days after his girlfriend tried to kill herself only fortuitously survived his own attempt. There is a "ripple" effect!

All this is not meant to suggest that the realization of a post-traumatic reaction is new; in 1917 Freud described what he called a physical trauma; we saw this as a process started by a threatening situation that is acute and overwhelming. He described this as a developmental sequence to trauma (1926). In 1985, Janoff-Bulman made the important observation that "much of the psychological trauma produced by victimizing events derives from the shattering of very basic assumptions that victims have held about the operation of the world." We all have constructs, a theory of the world, for example: "Johnny, the ten year old, doesn't kill himself." With the suicide, our view of the world may be shattered, resulting in possible PTSD. We have to cope with "Johnny killed himself."

Adjusting to a suicide is remarkably difficult. Freud (1939) distinguished between positive and negative effects of trauma. He saw remembering, repeating, and reexperiencing as positive, which is opposite of the more typical denial approach. Forgetting, avoidance, phobia, and inhibition were described by Freud as negative. These are common responses in many victims after a suicide, even in adults who are to guide our youngsters, such as principals, psychologists, etc. A common response is to deny it: "Don't talk about it; after all, talking about suicide causes suicide." We firmly believe, as has been so well documented with Vietnam victims, that this approach only exacerbates the trauma. However, as Wilson, Smith, and Johnson (1985) have pointed out, it is important for us to see that the victims of a suicide may be caught in a no-win cycle of events. They note the following:

> To talk about the powerful and overwhelming trauma means risking further stigmatization; the failure to discuss the traumatic episode increases the need for defensive avoidance and thus increases the probability of depression alternating with cycles of intensive imagery and other symptoms of PTSD. (p. 169)

We need to help survivors to work it through. We need to foster positive adjustive strategies..

It should be noted that PTSD is intended for adults; however, Eth and Pynoos (1985) have presented convincing arguments for applying it to children and adolescents. They note that children of trauma have exhibited such symptoms as "deleterious effects on cognition (including memory, school performance, and learning), affect, interpersonal relations, impulse control, and behavior, vegetative function, and the formulation of symptoms" (p. 41). Terr (1979), and Lifton and Olson (1976) have observed in studies of abducted children and in children surviving a disaster (e.g., Hiroshima) that there is a post-traumatic reaction and that, indeed, there are amazing commonalities in how children respond to various unusual trauma. Bowlby (1977) has made a number of observations about traumatic reactions to loss, notably anxious attachment behavior. Often children do not appear to be exhibiting a reaction (e.g., there are few recognizable overt verbalizations), but there may well be a negative reaction that could be fostered by an adult who also wants to deny the loss. Anna Freud (1966) noted that children often rely on various forms of denial, evident in fantasy, action, and affect, all to ease (numb) the pain.

One of the authors recalls working with a school-aged child who found his teenage brother hanging; he simply did not believe it—it did not happen. A child may sit for hours in front of a dead parent without responding. Denial may not be the only reaction. Aggressiveness, obsessive fantasies (recurrence), anxious arousal, behavioral problems, poor peer relations, school failure, and even imitation have been documented in children and adolescents after a suicide. For example, one eight year old was found scratching himself with a knife in his classroom, reacting to his teenage brother's serious attempt six months earlier. The reaction may not be immediate. One of the authors saw a teenager for therapy four years after one of the children for whom she frequently babysat had killed himself. She recurrently imagined that if only she was babysitting that night she could have saved the boy.

Despite commonalities in young peoples response to a trauma, Eth and Pynoos (1985) in their studies of children who saw a parent killed, noted that differences exist related to developmental age. In response to a suicide, we too must consider developmental lines. Erickson (1932) has pointed out that there are differences in how one responds to a crisis depending on one's developmental age. Newman (1976) has noted that in adolescents, their post-traumatic symptoms more and more resemble adult symptoms, especially post-traumatic acting out, truancy, precocious sexual actions, substance abuse, and delinquency. Anna Freud (1966) has suggested that such behaviors are defensive mechanisms and Nagara (1970) has postulated that much has to do with identifying with the victim (e.g., the suicide). These symptoms are ways of adjusting to the trauma; yet, they are not adaptive.

There are differences in the ways individuals respond to a trauma. Wilson, Smith, and Johnson (1985) have found in various survivor groups that one needs "to specify how the nature and complexity of the stressor event impacts on the unique personality of the survivor" (p. 167–8). In the same vein, it is important to realize that not all survivors of suicide are alike; they bring with them their own serial way of adjusting to a trauma (Shneidman 1985). It is unreasonable to believe that the psychological distress produced by suicide will produce the same effect in everyone. We have found that the closest "objects"—family, boy/girlfriend, close friend—are most at risk. We have, however, found people with PTSD who were distant (though maybe not psychologically) from the suicide. One recurrent marker appears to be if they had very seriously contemplated and/or attempted suicide themselves or if they knew someone who had killed himself. In one case, for example, the person most at immediate risk was the principal at a school—his parents had killed (homicide-suicide) themselves. In another case, the teacher had been suicidal for years. In general, however, Wilson and colleagues (1985) suggest that the more severe and complex the stressful life event, the greater the likelihood that an individual might develop symptoms of PTSD. All this suggests that anyone might be the client.

There have been a number of special programs developed for use soon after a particular trauma; e.g., prisoners of war, Iranian hostages, rape victims. Scurfield (1985) has noted that such intervention (postvention) appears to have a positive effect in preventing and lessening the severity of PTSD. Figley (1983) has suggested that the critical question is the following: Is the environment supportive? Or not?

Although there are individual differences, Green, Wilson, and Lindy (1985) have noted "the social environment may contribute to a person's recovery." There is most likely an interaction between person and event. Social supports are critical. As Green and colleagues (1985) note the "more supportive environments tend to be associated with better adjustment to stress" (p. 61). It is unfortunate that even in our schools adults foster denial and unwittingly promote negative adjustment. We believe that positive response needs to begin with the school administration, followed by school staff and other involved adult individuals. We can learn from the best known victims of PTSD, Vietnam veterans. Their PTSD was so severe because the general attitude toward Vietnam was so negative ("the war was a loss").

Review of the Literature

Our review of the literature produced only two published papers in suicide postvention in schools—including one of our own (Lamb and Dunne-Maxim

1987; Leenaars 1985). However, at recent conferences of the American Association of Suicidology, this topic has obtained increasing attention; in fact, a half-day program was set aside for the topic in Atlanta, Georgia in 1986, with the senior author chairing those sessions.

School postvention programs represent the organized response of a caring, humanistic institution to the traumatic loss of a student in such a way that the emotional needs of those remaining are dealt with effectively (Pelej and Scholzen 1987). Further, they are designed to forestall possible psychological damage within our framework of PTSD and facilitate grief resolution (Lamb and Dunne-Maxim 1987). Addressing the contagion or copy-cat effect by preventing suicide role modeling represents a primary concern (Lamartine-Anderson and Sattem 1986).

Zinner (1986) discusses the need for promoting "functional interpretation" of the loss, i.e., is there group concensus of what happened and why it happened; and "functional consequence," i.e., the idea that the school can be helped to make meaning of the suicidal death and provide a sense of closure and completion.

Leenaars and Wenckstern (1986) believe preplanned postvention efforts should be embedded within prevention efforts to aid in addressing suicide as an increasingly identified problem among our youth.

What is striking about the programs cited herein is the high rate of agreement regarding the structure or format of such programs. There is most controversy in regard to content issues and specifics.

Leenaars and Wenckstern (1986), and Lamb and Dunne-Maxim (1987) have advocated the need for a coordinator to take charge and to provide structure in such highly charged, traumatic situations. The development of a task force or team to head postvention efforts has been advocated in a similar vein (Lane-Malbon 1986; Pelej and Scholzen 1987). Some difference of opinion exists regarding whether the coordinator and/or consulting team should be "outside experts" (recommended by Lamb and Dunne-Maxim 1987) who serve to legitimize the school's response and are viewed as objective and neutral; or should be "inside personnel" (suggested by Pelej and Scholzen 1987) in the sense of not relying "upon experts from afar."

The importance of having a sound policy/plan for schools in place before a suicide occurs has been well documented by Comstock (1985), Lamartine-Anderson and Sattem (1986), Lamb and Dunne-Maxim (1987), Lane-Malbon (1986), and Leenaars (1985). Pre-arranged cooperation with law enforcement agencies and/or fire department and county coroner has been suggested by Pelej and Scholzen (1987).

The need for early group and individual crisis intervention has been clearly addressed (Lamb and Dunne-Maxim 1987; Leenaars 1985; Zinner 1986).

A school consultation and/or planning meeting is usually proposed as the first order of business in addressing the crisis after a suicide and is conducted as soon as possible after notification of the suicide (Comstock 1985; Lamartine-Anderson and Sattem 1986; Lamb and Dunne-Maxim 1987; Leenaars 1985; and Schulman 1986).

Consultations with school staff, including but not limited to, the teaching staff to prepare them in responding to students have been proposed by Leenaars and Wenckstern (1986). Pelej and Scholzen (1987) more strongly call for a mandatory staff meeting to address the issue of suicide and go over the day's planned events. Lamb and Dunne-Maxim (1987) have made it a "guiding principle" that the students cannot be helped until the faculty is helped. They utilize a structured group format in working with both staff and students and describe the consultants major task as helping faculty members with their own feelings about the suicide as well as teaching them how to be helpful to their students in turn. The authors explain that their structured group process as a technique "combines effective and cognitive material in a way that is neither overwhelming in its emotionality or so dryly intellectual as to lose the audience."

Carter and Brooks (1986) responded to a request for suicide postvention at a high school in their district by conducting a time-limited therapy program for the immediate survivor peer group, i.e., over a two-month period, within their clinical setting.

. Another, more common approach is the provision or conducting of staff, student, and parent workshops/seminars shortly after a suicide where the focus is primarily an educative one, and hence, reflects a preventive aspect of the program, though working through basic grief reactions is also encouraged. (Lamartine-Anderson and Sattem 1986; Lane-Malbon 1986; Leenaars and Wenckstern 1986).

Identification of the immediate survivor group (Lamb and Dunne-Maxim 1987; Zinner 1986) and of high risk students in general—whether they are at risk due to feelings of intense guilt at having missed a "clue," kept a fatal secret, or are suicidal themselves—has been strongly advocated as a critical aspect of any comprehensive program (Lamb and Dunne-Maxim 1987; Lamartine-Anderson and Sattem 1986; Lane-Malbon 1986; Pelej and Scholzen 1987; and Schulman 1986). Pelej and Scholzen (1987) have also identified the need to identify high risk school staff.

Providing assessment and/or counseling to individuals at risk at any point during postvention efforts and beyond, if needed, has been articulated by Lane-Malbon (1986) and Leenaars (1985). Establishing support groups such as student survivor support groups has been proposed by Lamartine-Anderson and Sattem (1986); Lane-Malbon (1986); and Pelej and Scholzen (1987). Peer counseling support groups have also been suggested (Lamartine-Anderson and Sattem 1986; Lane-Malbon 1986).

At every point within a postvention program or model, networking and linkage with community agencies are viewed as critical elements (Comstock 1985; Lane-Malbon 1986; Leenaars and Wenckstern 1986; Pelej and Scholzen, 1987). As Comstock (1985) has pointed out ". . . the crisis associated with a cluster of adolescent suicides is not just school business. Multiple agencies, mental health professionals, and virtually all residents should be involved."

The importance of an academic autopsy and consultation with colleagues has also been addressed (Leenaars 1985; Pelej and Scholzen 1987; Shulman 1986; Zinner 1986).

An increasing concern is how to deal effectively with the media. It has been proposed by several authors that a media policy should be formulated, again, before a suicide crisis develops, which clearly defines areas of responsibility, e.g., who should act as media spokesperson, etc. (Comstock 1985; Lamb and Dunne-Maxim 1987; Lamartine-Anderson and Sattem 1986).

As mentioned earlier, more agreement than disagreement has been noted by those proposing postvention programs for schools. However, there appears to be some controversy about more concrete, content issues. For example, for those who have talked about school assemblies as a forum to carry out postvention programs, Leenaars (1985) proposed that it is appropriate to hold small school assemblies (approximately 35 to 50 people). Lamartine-Anderson and Sattem (1986) stated that depending upon the size of the school, it is appropriate to hold assemblies for entire grade levels or even for all students.

Shulman (1986) proposed a general assembly for what he calls "fact clarification." Lamb and Dunne-Maxim (1987) have argued that for their program, large assemblies are just that, too large, too unmanageable for most professionals and not a good place for "processing." Pelej and Scholzen (1987) have argued strongly that one should "not empower the death by cancelling classes or disrupting the schedule of the school (e.g., holding special assemblies)."

The question of whether or not one should hold special events in memory of the deceased—seen as appropriate by Lamartine-Anderson and Sattem (1986) or as inappropriate as discussed by Lamb and Dunne-Maxim (1987)—is another example of where opinions differ.

As school postvention programs expand and emerge out of their infancy, it may be possible that systematic evaluation of the merits, strengths, and weaknesses of programs and their facilitators may at some point provide some basis for making more effective judgments regarding these issues/concerns. A recent attempt has been made in this direction as reported by Valente, Saunders, and Street (1986). As they have noted, controversy surrounds the "purpose, curriculum, and evaluation programs." They suggested some guidelines and issues for program evaluation including the following: training issues such as trainee/trainer selection procedures, evaluation, qualifications; data collection such as data about suicide behavior before and after programming; bereavement such as support services available, referral, monitoring; ethical and legal issues such as confidentiality of students and student records; program evaluation; community integration and resources; services delivery such as looking at or evaluating outreach, follow-up record keeping; assessment and intervention such as intervention skill and attitude, responses to survivors, accurate statistics.

The Model

Our postvention efforts are essentially a combination of educational strategies largely gleaned from the American Association of Suicidology; consultation intervention drawn in part from Goodstein (1978) and Watzlawick, Beavin, and Jackson (1967); crisis intervention strategies from Farberow (1967), Hoff (1984), Parad (1965), Shneidman (1980, 1985); and a few specifically related to trauma response, i.e., Lifton (1969) and Lindemann (1944); and especially postvention strategies from Shneidman (1981). Shneidman has given us some principles of postvention that are largely based on his extensive work with survivors in a psychotherapeutic context. They are ubiquitous (common) in understanding the event.

Our postvention program includes the following aspects; modifications may be necessary depending on such factors as time, situation, and nature of the suicide:

1) *Consultation*—Discussion, coordination, and planning are undertaken at every phase beginning with administration, followed by school staff, and then other involved individuals such as pupils and parents. Peer consultation and review among professional staff who are involved in the postvention program is undertaken to review the actions that have been taken and to plan/coordinate further action.

2) *Education*—Information about suicide—e.g. clues, myths, causes, what to do, where to go for help, etc.—is provided through discussion, seminars, workshops, small assemblies (35 to 50 people) at the school and within the community.

3) *Crisis Intervention*—Emergency/crisis response is provided utilizing basic problem-solving strategies. We believe that pupils and staff of the local school will most likely need support when dealing with a suicide crisis. It is crucial not to underestimate the closeness of relationships nor the intensity of reactions of individuals who are experiencing a post-traumatic reaction.

4) *Community Linkage*—We believe that it is imperative that survivors of

suicide be provided with the appropriate support. We have developed a network to aid in making referrals to appropriate community service(s), and to exchange information with and coordinate our services with appropriate community services as needed.

5) *Assessment and Counseling*—Our own mandate calls for providing evaluation and therapy as needed or when requested by the school principal.

6) Follow-up—Periodic follow-ups are undertaken with the school principal, school staff, and psychological and social work services staff. A formal final consultation several months after the suicide is provided to give a formal closure to the program. However, every attempt is made to let all concerned know that we are available for follow-up if the need arises.

In the sense that postvention consists of those activities that serve to reduce the after effects of the traumatic event in the lives of survivors, it serves to address PTSD. It also addresses the contagion effect (ripple or copycat effect), which is a well-documented phenomenon (Phillips and Carstensen 1986). The Yukiko Okada incident is one example. Even in children we can see such an effect; we recall an eight-year-old boy who attempted to kill himself in the fashion of his teenage brother's attempt.

The emotional and psychological vulnerability of our children and adolescents related to issues such as strong identification with the peer group, susceptibility to imitation, and role modeling increases the risk of these survivors imitating the event. In fact, after the suicide of a child in our school system, we have experienced a number of other children exhibiting PTSD. This has also been the case when a pupil has attempted suicide; others have expressed suicidal ideation or attempted in a similar manner. As part of any postvention effort, particularly within a school system, it is important to identify those who are now at a greater risk for PTSD. It is reported that survivors of a suicide, for example, have a 300 percent greater chance of attempting than those who have not directly experienced the loss of someone through suicide.

Principles of Postvention —derived from Shneidman but modified for application within a school setting:

1. In working with the survivors victims of suicide, it is best to begin as soon as possible after the tragedy, within the first 24 hours if that can be managed with children at school. It is networking between all personnel—administrators, teachers, special services staff—that is so critical at this stage (not only when initiating the program). It is helpful to provide intervention with survivors as soon as possible and particu-

larly prior to funeral arrangements. Schools, for example, require the early actions of professionals to help bring the appearance of strength and reassurance to a situation that is unanticipated and overwhelming. Early intervention can facilitate the planning of created group rituals that can be combined with formal funeral ceremonies that allow children to acknowledge their relationship to the deceased and be a part of culturally prescribed leave-taking rituals.

2. Resistance may be met from the survivors; some—but not all—are willing or even eager to have the opportunity to talk to professionally-oriented persons. Others only wish to deny the event (a negative reaction). In our own attempts, we have been fortunate to receive the cooperation of parents, who play a critical, indirect role in our efforts in the school. A book recommended to us by a number of survivors of suicide as being helpful is *After Suicide* by John H. Hewett (1980). Hewett tells survivors that each of them will be tempted to withdraw into their individual shells and mourn alone. The jealousies and hard feelings that existed before the suicide "throws a triple whammy" on each survivor. First, a member in the family has been lost. Second, the pain and shock of a sudden death will be experienced. Third, each survivor has to deal with the fact that it was suicide with concommittant pain and regret. To combat this tendency to withdraw from all the pain and confusion, Hewett urges family members (including child family members) to keep the channels of love and communication open—to talk to one another, to touch at every opportunity, to weep and rage and keep silence together.

Hewett reminds the reader of the root origin of the word survive which comes from two Latin words; "super," which means "over," and "vivere," which means "to live." The survivor has a chance to start over or to continue to live a life that he/she might well have felt to be over. Although the PTSD patterns in a school system are different in many ways, we have observed notable similarities with Hewett's description of the surviving family. The survivors at the school need to learn to go on living—to work, to play.

Prior to this step, within a school setting, it is important to identify the survivors. Unless the group tends to be small and homogeneous, it can be expected that some subgroups within the larger context may be more affected by the suicide than others, e.g., the actual classmate's of the deceased as opposed to other more distant classes/grades in the school. At times it is difficult to identify all survivors at risk. We have already cited the case where the principal, whose own parents had killed themselves, was most at risk. In our experience, once the survivors—potential PTSD victims—have been identified, many of them have been very willing and relieved to have an opportunity to talk about the tragedy and their cognitions, feelings, etc. Taking care of those identified as survivors reassures others, e.g., the more distant members of the group, that appropriate and beneficial or salutary actions have been forthcoming.

3. Negative emotions about the decedent (the deceased person) or about death itself—irritation, anger, envy, shame, guilt, and so on—need to be explored, but not necessarily at the very beginning. Timing is so important. It is our experience that this is true whether one is dealing in a one-to-one therapeutic situation as therapist and patient or as a professional who is assisting individuals and/or groups in a school setting.

4. The postvener should play the important role of reality tester. He/she is not so much the echo of conscience as the quiet voice of reason. Again, within a school setting it is very important to provide survivors, especially children, with sound adult role models to guide and assist them through the PTSD process.

5. Referral to community services may be crucial in some cases. One should be constantly alert for symptoms of PTSD, such as possible decline in physical health and in overall mental well-being.

As stated earlier, networking among service providers is important as we believe it is imperative that survivors of suicide be made aware of and provided with appropriate support. It is simply not the school alone that needs to respond but other services too—bereavement services, community crisis services, clergy, family doctor, etc. Post-traumatic stress is itself a dire process, almost akin to a disease in that there are subtle factors at work that can take a heavy toll unless they are treated and controlled. In the case of suicide, not only do survivors need to cope with the death of a loved one or of a friend but also with the emotional aspects of a death that was caused by one's own hand, such as anger, feelings of betrayal and/or rejection, loss, guilt, and shame coupled with a human need to understand and make meaning of what often may be hindered by their developmental level—notably their understanding of death (Pfeffer 1986).

6. Needless to say, pollyannish optimism or banal platitudes should be avoided; statements such as "Don't worry, Sally, this too shall pass," or "You'll get over it," or "Everything will be okay, Billy, now run out and play," are in no way helpful. Survivors find these kinds of statements not helpful, and they may be PTSD enhancing. Providing an atmosphere of compassionate understanding without being judg-

mental in any way is more helpful. One must be a good listener to be helpful.

7. PTSD work takes a while—from several months to the end of the life, but certainly more than three weeks or six sessions. Our efforts in the school typically last about three to four months (although individual cases may be longer). One always leaves the door open. There are no definite (or specific) changes to grief as espoused by Kubler-Ross and others. There are no stages as predictable as $1 + 1 = 2$ to PTSD. The point here is that within our framework the length of session cannot be arbitrarily prescribed. Similarly, with a survivor it is not six months, ten months and so on. To illustrate: two years after a young boy killed himself, his sister required therapy when she reached the same age as when her brother killed himself—not an uncommon phenomenon among siblings. Research shows our society sanctions an acceptable mourning period of approximately one year with fairly well-known rituals that mark the beginning and end of mourning. (Although we know of one case where a woman in her fifties was lambasted by her mother—who is in her eighties—for going to a dance at a club with a widowed girlfriend. This was Maria's first social outing since her husband's death eight years earlier.) There is no simple rule of thumb with regard to the PTSD process. PTSD, instead, is a very individual process and if partially or not worked through and/or resolved, may take considerably longer and in some cases to the end of life as Shneidman indicates. For children survivors, the suicide of someone very near and dear may indeed leave irreversible scars for life depending on such factors as that child's level of cognitive, emotional, and psychological development.

8. A comprehensive program of health care on the part of a benign and enlightened community should include preventive, interventive, and postventive elements.

Table 1 presents the basic principles.

Table 1
Principles of Postvention

1. In working with survivor victims of suicide, it is best to begin as soon as possible after the tragedy—within the first 24 hours if that can be managed—with children at the school.
2. Resistance may be met from the survivors; some—but not all—are either willing or eager to have the opportunity to talk to professionally-oriented persons.
3. Negative emotions about the decedent (the deceased person) or about the death itself—irritation,

anger, envy, shame, guilt, and so on—need to be explored, but not at the very beginning. Timing is so important.

4. The postvener should play the important role of reality tester. He/she is not so much the echo of conscience as *the quiet voice of reason.*
5. Referral to community services may be crucial in some cases. One should be constantly alert for possible decline in physical health and in overall mental well-being.
6. Needless to say, pollyannish optimism, or banal platitudes should be avoided.
7. PTSD takes a while—from several months to the end of life, but certainly more than three weeks or six sessions.
8. A comprehensive program of health care on the part of a benign and enlightened community should include preventive, interventive, *postventive* elements.

Case Illustration

Next, we will attempt to illustrate our program with a suicide case utilizing a time sequence format.

1. The coordinator was notified of the pupil's suicide on the evening of his death by the school superintendent of the pupil's school. Telephone consultations were undertaken that evening with administration, school principal, and classroom teacher to pre-plan a cooperative effort at the school the next day.

2. The following morning, the principal and the coordinator discussed appropriate responses with the entire school staff including teachers, teacher's aides, secretary, janitor, etc., to possible questions and reactions since many children and parents were aware of the incident before school started. They were urged to be open about the suicide without in any way being sensational in the hope of providing sound models for the children. Individual support and encouragement were provided to the pupil's classroom teacher who was in shock and was feeling somewhat guilty about whether he had missed a suicidal clue. The coordinator held individual discussions with other school staff including (most important because easily overlooked) the secretary's responses on the telephone. Further direct consultations by psychological and social work (Special Services) staff were provided to school staff during the day following the suicide and in the next few months as requested or as a need was perceived.

3. Involved personnel of Special Services undertook a group consultation the day following the suicide to review the actions that had been taken and to coordinate further action. Further peer consultations were undertaken by Special Services staff as the program continued since it is our belief that such postvention should not be undertaken by one individual alone, thus preventing stress overload and providing ongoing coverage

as well as a number of contacts and supports for the individual(s) in crisis. Our experience has also shown that such consultations and reviews should be supportive (e.g., "What did you do?"; "What other things might have been considered?"; "What can we do next?"; etc.) and not assaultive., i.e., overly critical (e.g. "Did you do———?"; "Why did/didn't you do———?"; etc.) to be helpful not only to the providers of the service but the program as well.

4. The coordinator arranged a consultation with the deceased pupil's parents, mainly per their request. Time was spent discussing their feelings, thoughts, and behavior as well as the reactions of their adolescent daughter. Therapy was recommended for their daughter who appeared to be overly denying the death until the first family outing, which resulted in her reacting by crying uncontrollably and expressing verbal anger toward her parents—PTSD symptoms. The recommendation for counseling was subsequently followed and counseling assistance was provided by our own staff at the girl's school. The parents were also referred to a survivor group provided in our community by a service agency. We believe it is imperative that survivors of suicide be provided with the appropriate support. Thus, we assist these individuals to obtain such services. However, despite this community service in our city, we believe that the pupils and staff at the local school are likely to need support in response to a suicide crisis. One should not underestimate the closeness of relations nor the intensity of reactions of individuals undergoing PTSD. Further contacts have occurred with the suicide's family (even three years later) at their request and they are aware that further consultations are available.

5. The coordinator undertook consultations with the parents of several classmates when requested. As a result, several referrals were made to our psychological services and social work services and other community agencies. We believe that such supportive service is essential. For example, one classmate continued to have disturbing dreams about the suicide six months after the death.

6. During the week of the suicide the coordinator organized and presented an educational workshop to the school staff to inform them about suicide among young people and about suicide prevention services available in our system and community.

7. Staff organized and presented a workshop about "Death, Dying, and Suicide" to the children and the teacher in the pupil's classroom. All parents were informed about the workshop and its general purpose and, as we have increasingly found, all the parents consented to have their child included in the program. The purposes of the workshop included

the following: to deal with the children's reactions to suicide and death generally, their guilt feelings, their previous unresolved grief and their other reaction patterns, as well as to give the children an opportunity to discuss the suicide openly and frankly in a supportive fashion—all to address the possibility of the PTSD syndrome.

8. Periodic follow-up with the principal, school staff, Psychological Services and Social Work Services staff were undertaken. The coordinator undertook a final consultation four months after the suicide with the principal, classroom teacher, and Special Services staff to provide a formal close to the postvention program although "the doors were left open" to the school; we strongly believe that the potential for contact for an indefinite extended period should be included in any crisis intervention program. We found this informal discussion important not only for our own educational purposes and professional development but because it also assisted us in the review of the program's effectiveness.

Postvention in school may not only include a student, but a parent (or even a teacher). The following is a case example.

1. Telephone consultation between the principal and the coordinator regarding immediate questions, course of action, etc., was immediately undertaken upon notification. Following the telephone consult, the principal met with his staff, notifying them about the suicide. Staff were encouraged to respond in a calm, matter-of-fact manner with concern and compassion if a pupil wanted to discuss the event.
2. The coordinator met with the principal, the teachers, and other interested staff the following afternoon to discuss approaches, responses to children's questions, their feelings and reactions, PTSD symptoms, what to look for, as well as to disseminate information about where to get help within our city.
3. Psychological and Social Work Services were initiated as needed. The three children whose parent had suicided were given particular care when they returned to class, making sure that necessary services were provided, not only in the school.
4. Follow-up consultations by the coordinator were undertaken as needed.

We have come to learn that system—more accurately an individual's, e.g., principal's, denial of the event/trauma—may hinder a response. The following is an example.

1. The coordinator was notified of the pupil's suicide.

2. That same day, the coordinator and other staff met with the vice-principal to assess the situation and to implement the appropriate intervention plan. By this time the school staff had already arranged, without consultation, a meeting with students in the classes of which the deceased student had been a classmate—an unfortunate first deviation of the model. One follows the structure and does not implement one's own program!

3. Despite reluctance, the consultants had no choice but to meet with the students. As previously outlined, attempts were made to begin discussions with the students with an understanding that follow-up, as our model calls for, would be provided.

4. The next day, the principal stopped all response, saying that it would only aggravate the situation—"After all, we don't want to put ideas in their heads"—even the follow-up wasn't allowed.

This case highlights the critical need to have a model for suicide postvention in schools. A number of serious attempts followed at that school—the contagion effect that postvention is designed to address, occurred. Even years later, there has been "fall out" at that school. We need to stress in our schools the need to respond; *a principal or other school administrator simply should not be allowed to make the decision.* There is not only a need to respond positively to the possible PTSD reaction but also to obvious liability issues. To address this often encountered "system" concern, we suggest that we begin in establishing a postvention project with upper administration, followed by lower administration and school staff, and other involved individuals.

Conclusion

Suicide occurs and although most of us will never experience such an event, it is important that we all increase our knowledge. We need to learn to respond positively to such a trauma, not deny the event. Development of suicide postvention in school systems is a critical force in these efforts. School staff need to develop postvention skills to address PTSD. In this chapter we have attempted to outline such a model, providing framework (PTSD) to understand the event, a review of the literature, an outline for a postvention model and case presentation to illustrate our model. We believe that our most important future endeavour is evaluation.

We know of many school staff who have saved a life. All of us have a role in addressing PTSD when it occurs. The belief that suicide postvention is only temporary is a myth. With appropriate help, individuals can be helped through trauma (suicide, disaster, etc). Maybe the words of Dr. James O. Wells

(1987)—one of the psychologists who addressed the *Challenger* disaster in Christa McAuliffe's home school—may provide hope:

The crisis of disaster can be an opportunity to learn from experience and to form the relationships which may be tapped in future crisis.

References

American Psychiatric Association. 1980. *Diagnostic and statistical manual of mental disorders.* 3rd ed. Washington, DC: American Psychiatric Association.

Bowlby, J. 1977. The making and breaking of affectionate bonds. *British Journal of Psychiatry* 130: 201–208 and 421–31.

Carter, B.C. and A. Brooks. 1986. An exploration of group postvention techniques. Paper presented at the conference of the American Association of Suicidology, Atlanta, Georgia.

Comstock, B.S. 1985. Youth suicide cluster: A community response. In the American Association of Suicidology *Newslink.*

Domino, G. and A.A. Leenaars. (in press). Attitudes toward suicide: A comparison of Canadian and United States College Students. *Suicide and Life-Threatening Behavior.*

Erickson, E. 1932. *The life cycle completed:* New York: W.W. Norton.

Eth, G., and R. Pynoos. 1985. Developmental perspective on psychic trauma in childhood. In C. Figley, ed. *Trauma and Its Wake.* New York: Brunner/Mazel.

Farberow, N. 1967. Crisis, disaster, and suicide: Theory and therapy. In E. Shneidman, ed. *Essays in self-destruction* . New York: Science House, Inc.

Figley, C., ed. 1978. *Stress disorders among Vietnam veterans.* New York: Brunner/Mazel.

Figley, C. 1983. Catastrophes: An overview of family reactions: In C. Figley and H. Cubbin, eds. *Coping with Catastrophes.* Vol. 2 of *Stress and the Family.* New York: Brunner/Mazel.

———1985. Introduction. In C. Figley, ed. *Trauma and its wake.* New York: Brunner/Mazel.

Freud, A. 1966. *Ego and mechanism of defense.* New York: International Universe.

Freud, S. 1917. Introductory lectures in psychoanalysis. Vol. 16 of J. Strachery, ed. *The standard edition of the complete psychological work of S. Freud.* London, England: Hogarth.

———(1917b). *Mourning and melancholia.* Vol. 14.

———(1926). *Inhibitions, symptoms, and anxiety.* Vol. 20.

———(1939). *Moses and Monotheism.* Vol. 23.

Gleser, G., B. Green and C. Wignet. 1981. *Buffalo Creek revisited: Prolonged psychosocial effects of disaster.* New York: Simon and Schuster.

Goodstein, L. 1978. *Consulting with human service systems.* Menlo Park, CA: Addison-Wesley.

Green, B., J. Wilson and J. Lindy. 1985. Conceptualizing post-traumatic stress disorders. A psychosocial framework. In Figley, ed. *Trauma and its wake.* New York: Brunner/Mazel.

Hewett, J. 1980. *After suicide.* Philadelphia: Westminster.

Hoff, L. 1984. *People in crisis.* 2nd ed. Menlo Park, CA: Addison-Wesley.

Horowitz, M. 1979. Psychological response to serious life events. In V. Hamilton and D. Warburton, eds. *Humor stress and cognition.* New York: Wiley.

Janoff-Bulman, R. 1985. The aftermath of victimization: Rebuilding shattered assumptions. In C. Figley, ed. *Trauma and its wake.* New York: Brunner/Mazel.

Lamartine, C.E. 1985. Suicide prevention in educational settings: After a suicide death. Pamphlet put out by the Suicide Prevention Center, Inc., Dayton, Ohio.

Lamartine-Anderson, C. and L. Sattem. 1986. After a suicide in an educational setting. Paper presented at the conference of the American Association of Suicidology, Atlanta, Georgia.

Lamb, F. and K. Dunne-Maxim. 1987. Postvention in schools: Policy and process. In E. Dunne, J. McIntosh and K. Dunne-Maxim, eds. *Suicide and its aftermath: Understanding and counseling the survivors.* New York: W.W. Norton.

Lane-Malbon, L. 1986. After suicide: Crisis intervention in the school. Paper presented at the conference of the American Association of Suicidology, Atlanta, Georgia.

Leenaars, A.A. 1985. Suicide postvention in a school system. *Canada's Mental Health* 33 (4).

———1988. *Suicide notes.* New York: Human Sciences.

Leenaars, A.A. and S. Wenckstern. 1986. Suicide postvention in a school system. Paper presented at the conference of the American Association of Suicidology, Atlanta, Georgia.

Lifton, R. 1969. *Death in life: Survivors of Hiroshima.* New York: Vintage.

Lifton, R. and E. Olson. 1976. The human meaning of total disaster: The Buffalo Creek experience. *Psychiatry* 39:1–18

Lindemann, E. 1944. Symptomatology and management of acute grief. *American Journal Psychiatry* 101: 141–148.

Nagara, H. 1970. Children's reactions to the death of important objects: A developmental approach. *Psychoanalytic Study of the Child* 25: 360–500.

Newman, C.J. 1976. Children of disaster: Clinical observations at Buffalo Creek. *American Journal of Psychiatry 133*::306–12.

Parad, H., ed. 1965. *Crisis intervention: Selected readings.* New York: Family Service Association of America.

Pelej, J.P. and K.C. Scholzen. 1987. Postvention: A school's response to a suicide. Paper presented at the conference of the American Association of Suicidology, San Francisco, California.

Pfeffer, C. 1986. *Suicidal behavior in children.* New York: Guilford.

Phillips, D. 1986. Effect of the media. Paper presented at the conference of the American Association of Suicidology, Atlanta, Georgia.

Phillips, D. and M. Carstensen. 1986. Clustering of teenage suicides after television news stories about suicide. *New England Journal of Medicine 315*:685–89.

Scurfield, R. 1985. Post-trauma stress assessment and treatment. Overview and formulation. In C. Figley, ed. *Trauma and its wake.* New York: Brunner/Mazel.

Shneidman, E. 1973. Suicide. *Encyclopedia Britannica.* Chicago: William Benton.

———1980. Psychotherapy with suicidal patients. In E. Shneidman, ed. *Suicide thoughts and reflections, 1960-1980.* New York: Human Sciences.

———1981. Postvention: The care for the bereaved. In E. Shneidman *Suicide thoughts and reflections.* New York: Human Sciences.

———(1983). Postvention and the survivor-victim. *Deaths of man.* New York: Jason Aronsom.

———1985. *Definition of suicide.* New York: Wiley.

Shulman, N. 1986. Tragedy in Concord: Crisis intervention in a school following a student fatality. In the American Association of Suicidology *Newslink.*

Terr, L. 1979. Children of Chonchilla: Study of psychic trauma. *Psychoanalytic Study of the Child* 34:547–623.

Valente, S.M., J.M. Saunders and R. Street. 1986. Adolescent bereavement programs in the schools. Paper presented at the conference of the American Association of Suicidology, Atlanta, Georgia.

Watzlawick, P., J. Beavin and D. Jackson. 1967. *Pragmatics of human communication.* New York: W.W. Norton.

Wells, J. 1982. The community in crisis. Paper presented at the conference of the National Council of Community Mental Health Centers, June Miami, Florida.

Wilson, J., W. Smith and S. Johnson. 1985. A comparative analysis of PTSD among various survivor groups. In C. Figley, ed. *Trauma and its wake.* New York: Brunner/Mazel.

Zinner, E.S. 1986. Survivor intervention strategy in the suicide of a sixth-grader. Paper presented at the conference of the American Association of Suicidology, Atlanta, Georgia.